Validating Your Training

PRACTICAL TRAINER SERIES

Validating Your Training

TONY NEWBY

Amsterdam • Johannesburg • London
San Diego • Sydney • Toronto

First published in 1992 by Kogan Page, in association with the Institiute of Training and Development.

Kogan Page Limited
120 Pentonville Road
London N1 9JN

© Tony Newby, 1992

British Library Cataloguing in Publication Data

A CIP record for this book is available from the British Library.

ISBN 0 7494 0551 1

Published in the U.S. by
  Pfeiffer & Company
  8517 Production Avenue
  San Diego, CA 92121-2280
  (619) 578-5900
  FAX (619) 578-2042

Printed in the United States of America

ISBN 0 88390 342 3

Contents

Series Editor's Foreword *Roger Buckley*   7

Introduction   9
    Is this Book for You?   9
    The Roots of this Book   10
    What is Validation about?   10
    How to Use this Book   11
    Approach   11

1 Getting Started with Validation   13
    Why Validate Training?   13
    Is Validation Really Necessary?   15
    The Benefits of Validation   15
    Validation, Objectives and Competences 17
    Validation within the Training Design Process 17
    The Organizational Context   18
    Where do You Start?   20
    The Politics of Measuring Training   20
    How Much Validation do You Need?   21
    Designing the Validation Project   22
    Techniques Overview   28

2 Testing Knowledge   31
    Applications   31
    Resistance to Testing   32
    Types of Test Item   33
    Designing Tests – The Stages   34
    Recall (Supply) Items – Completion Items 37
    Recall (Supply) Items – Essay   38
    Recall (Supply) Items – Short Answer   39
    Recognition Items – Multiple-Choice Questions 39
    Recognition Items – True/False Questions 40

	Recognition Items Matching Items	41
3	**Testing Interpersonal Skills**	**43**
	Introduction	43
	Behaviour Observation Instruments	44
	Self-report Methods	53
	Validating Attitude Change by Repertory Grid	67
4	**Practical Tests**	**75**
	Introduction	76
	Classifying Skills for Testing	77
	Designing the Practical Test	83
5	**General Topics**	**88**
	Training for Behaviour Observation	88
	Training of Testers	90
	Training for Validation Interviewing	91
	Attitudes or Behaviour?	98
	Using End-of-course Reactions Data	99
6	**Statistical Issues in Validation**	**100**
	Why Statistics?	100
	Scientific Method	101
	Control Groups	101
	Sampling	104
	Analysing the Data	105
	Descriptive Statistics	107
	The Validation Report	108
	Statistics in Testing	110
	Notes	115
	Index	116

Series Editor's Foreword

Organizations get things done when people do their jobs effectively. To make this happen they need to be well trained. A number of people are likely to be involved in this training: identifying the needs of the organization and of the individual, selecting or designing appropriate training to meet those needs, delivering it and assessing how effective it was. It is not only 'professional' or full-time trainers who are involved in this process; personnel managers, line managers, supervisors and job holders are all likely to have a part to play.

This series has been written for all those who get involved with training in some way or another, whether they are senior personnel managers trying to link the goals of the organization with training needs or job holders who have been given responsibility for training newcomers. Therefore, the series is essentially a practical one which focuses on specific aspects of the training function. This is not to say that the theoretical underpinnings of the practical aspects of training are unimportant. Anyone seriously interested in training is strongly encouraged to look beyond 'what to do' and 'how to do it' and to delve into the areas of why things are done in a particular way.

The authors have been selected because they have considerable practical experience. All have shared, at some time, the same difficulties, frustrations and satisfactions of being involved in training and are now in a position to share with others some helpful and practical guidelines.

In this book Tony Newby provides sound guidelines on the use of reliable techniques that help us to answer those all-important questions about whether training has achieved its objectives and subsequently whether this has led to improved performance.

Validation of training is equally important as any other stage in the training cycle; in fact without it we do not have a complete cycle. Whilst there is a growing recognition of the need for validation, there are still questions in the minds of trainers about what validation actually is. Some of the techniques used still reflect elements of complacency and token gestures. The end of course questionnaire or 'happy sheet' have become so familiar and so much a feature of courses that their value has been taken for granted. Such techniques are of limited and of questionable reliability in giving us the answers that we need as trainers or as line managers. The application of the more rigorous techniques described here is certain to improve the effectiveness of validation and, as a result, the quality of training.

ROGER BUCKLEY

Introduction

Is this Book for You?

This is designed to be a practical 'how to do it' book. It spells out step-by-step how to use validation techniques in order to strengthen the effectiveness of training, to the benefit of the reader's organization. It quite specifically avoids academic debate, obscure footnotes, and recommendations for further reading.

The book has been written for the professional trainer, the personnel specialist and for the line manager who holds training responsibilities. Any competent person working in training should be able to use this book to design validation instruments which can be applied in his or her organization, with the object of:

– determining whether or not training has achieved what was intended;
– determining whether or not the methods adopted were effective;
– determining whether or not what was achieved through training was in fact useful in terms of enhancing work performance.

The validation techniques that are described here will be found useful not only for conventional courses but also for such learning activities as:

– kerbside conferences and other coaching opportunities;
– training that takes place within staff meetings;
– distance learning;
– management development;
– corporate communications events;
– problem-solving teams;
– computer-based training;
– action learning;

Any activity intended to improve people's capability to perform a work task can be validated; for simplicity, all such activities are referred to as 'training'.

The Roots of this Book

Back in the early 1970s, I had become indirectly conscious of the lack of validation in much training. On a number of occasions I had found myself on the receiving end of so-called 'training' which, behind clouds of obfuscation, proved to be literally purposeless.

Validation and evaluation of training became a significant professional issue for me in the latter 1970s. I felt dissatisfied with what was then available to the trainer. At that time I was fortunate to be part of an upsurge in serious vocational training in housing management, accompanied by research into training effectiveness. There was the opportunity to be involved in a number of pioneering research projects (notably with Marion Brion's team at the City University and subsequently, under Professor Herriot, at Birkbeck College). The combination of working in the academic world, in the public sector and in commercial organizations proved very fruitful and enabled me to develop the practical side of validation in ways that would be useful to people who design and deliver training.

What is Validation about?

The distinction between validation and evaluation does not stand up well to logical scrutiny. I have argued elsewhere that there is such a profusion of terminologies and conceptual models that it is best to call the whole range of processes 'evaluation' and then concentrate on the practicalities of each specific project.[1] The alternative tends to lead to paralysis through conceptual hair-splitting. That is, of course, a core activity for academia, but it does not carry much weight when you are trying to justify next year's training budget.

This book focuses exclusively upon 'validation', using it as a term that describes the range of processes by which the practitioner can assess how well or how badly one or another of the elements of training have worked. This definition therefore excludes consideration of questions about the value, or worthwhileness, of training which – conveniently though arbitrarily – I will here refer to as 'evaluation'.

How to Use this Book

Chapter 1 discusses a range of general issues, provides an overview of the different techniques and gives you a route map for setting up validation projects.

Chapters 2, 3 and 4 describe in detail how to design validation instruments using different techniques for different purposes:

- validating knowledge-based training
- validating interpersonal skills
- validating technical and commercial skills

Chapter 5 gathers together a number of topics that either apply to several techniques (and hence belong in no one technique chapter) or which would simply clutter the step-by-step design descriptions if they were included there.

Chapter 6 gathers together all the guidelines on statistical topics within validation. Certain kinds of validation information cannot be obtained unless statistical techniques are employed. These are not matters on which an intuitive judgement is feasible. Furthermore, appropriate use of statistical techniques is one (among several) measures which the practitioner can take in order to increase the methodological rigour of the validation study.

The statistical topics covered in Chapter 6 are:

- scientific method and validation;
- control groups;
- sampling;
- descriptive statistics;
- the validation report;
- statistics in testing: gain ratios; comparing groups; standard (Z) scores; comparing frequencies; guessing correction; reliability; validity; item analysis.

Approach

I have set out not only to explain how to use the techniques so that you can confidently design your own validation instruments, but have also tried to highlight some of the practical issues of organizational life and politics that can impinge on assessments of training.[2]

Each chapter begins with an outline summary of the content. Techniques are illustrated with examples and there are numerous practical tips, drawn from a decade and a half of close personal involvement in this specialist field.

I hope that you find this book easy to use – and useful when put into practice.

1 Getting Started with Validation

▷   SUMMARY   ◁

- The need for validation in training is explained and the benefits outlined. The links between validation, training objectives and competences are explained and you are shown how validation should be built into the training design process.
- Practical tips on getting started are described and the important issue of managing the organizational context and the politics of measuring training are examined. The chapter provides criteria for deciding how much validation is needed in your training. Full, step-by-step guidance is then provided on the design of the validation project and the chapter concludes with a brief overview of the techniques that are described in Chapters 2, 3 and 4.

Why Validate Training?

Training needs arise in one of two ways. Either:

- someone is not performing work tasks as effectively as they could, because of a deficiency of knowledge or skill,

or

- someone needs to learn new knowledge or skills in anticipation of some future change in the work he or she undertakes.

In both instances, training is used in the expectation that it will produce positive changes: people will do their jobs better. The purpose of validation is to test that assumption that training has an effect on people.

The central validation question is 'Did that training make a measurable difference?'. Depending on the context, the measurement may be more or less precise and the changes achieved may vary from very little to a great deal. The key point is that the question of *measurable difference* is raised – and merely anecdotal or 'happy sheet' feedback is relegated to the waste basket. Leading on from the central question of 'Did it work?', validation may also focus upon the related question of 'Why did the training work/not work?', which focuses less on the outcome and more on the processes of design and delivery of training. Finally, validation may loop back to the original diagnosis of need, to ask, 'Were the right issues addressed by the training?'.

It can be a useful exercise to review work tasks purely from the point of view of identifying performance shortfalls; then you can ask the second-level question, 'Are these deficiencies likely to respond to a training solution?' (Figure 1.1 gives you a framework for this). By starting out with clearly-identified performance problems, the task of validation is made comparatively straightforward.

EXAMPLES	HAPPENS HERE?	ESTIMATE OF LOSS £	TARGET IMPROVEMENT £
Customer complaints Equipment down-time Delivery delays Breakages Lost sales Accidents Quality failures Staff turnover Recruitment errors Ineffective training Uncontrolled overheads Bad debts Stock control problems *add your own examples*			

Figure 1.1 *Identifying performance deficiencies which may respond to training solutions*

Is Validation Really Necessary?

The question whether trainers or managers can do without validation of training needs to be asked, if only because it requires money, human resources and energy – and may mean less time for the delivery of training services to organizational clients.

There are always some limitations to what a validation study is able to achieve. Sometimes, these obstacles devalue the whole study. Validation is never quite as 'scientifically objective' as we might wish, especially if we base our position on a simplistic notion of the objectivity achieved by the physical sciences. On some occasions, corporate politics undermine the best-designed of studies.

On the other hand, some validation is usually better than no validation. Even methodologically-flawed studies are usually good enough for the purposes of making training policy decisions. Without some measurement of results, trainers and managers are in the position of running hard without knowing where the finishing line is – or even whether they are moving in the right direction.

The validation process itself yields benefits both for the training department and for the organization as a whole; it really does offer a win-win opportunity. Finally, and not least, if trainers do not attempt to validate their work others will do it for them.

The Benefits of Validation

Six direct benefits can be identified:

- *Quality control*, in the sense of whether a product or service is fit for the purpose. Applied to training as a service, that calls for an assessment of the extent to which changes in work performance can be demonstrated to arise from it. Good practices can be reinforced and less effective ones amended. Scarce training resources can then be reallocated to where they will do most good.
- *Efficient training design*: the process of setting training objectives and that of setting validation criteria by which that training can be measured form two sides of the same coin. The identification of measurement criteria or performance standards for the objective in turn encourages clear thinking about the elements of learning that will be needed. It also encourages a focus upon observable, behavioural changes rather than upon 'awareness' objectives.

Incidentally, it is invariably more economical of design time and usually yields better validation data when you build validation into training designs right from the start. The most expensive and inefficient option is to add validation on as a postscript after the training has been implemented.

● *Professional self-esteem*: systematic validation data give trainers a well-founded rather than intuitive assessment of their performance. This can be linked to the organization's appraisal system, where it offers a better alternative to less meaningful approximations to performance measures, such as number of training contact hours, or body counts of trainees, which measure effort rather than results.

● *Track record*: validation data collected over a period of time make it possible to demonstrate a track record of effective training, helpful when it comes to budget negotiations. However, this is not a crisis-response measure; experience suggests that it takes about an 18-month lead time to get a properly-devised system in place.

● *Appropriate criteria of assessment*: people make judgements about the training that they, or their subordinates, experience. In the absence of any formal validation system (and particularly if the organization relies on end-of-course 'happy sheets') the kinds of assessment that people will make are very predictable: trainees will typically respond in terms of their 'enjoyment'; managers in terms of days lost from work by their staff; and accountants will make inter-firm comparisons such as the 'cost per trainee' or the number of 'training days' provided. Whether trainers like it or not, judgements about the effectiveness of training are made. Formalised validation pre-empts judgements on inappropriate criteria.

● *Intervention strategy*: validation can be used to change the way that training fits into the organization. It provides an opportunity (sometimes fiercely resisted) for trainers and managers to examine and redefine their respective roles in the training process. In turn, the training department gets to play a more active policy role, whilst managerial cooperation opens the doors to better diagnosis of training needs.

If training is to make a real contribution to corporate success it cannot operate in a vacuum. Trainers should resist putting 'keep out' signs around their territory because effective training is a partnership of complementary roles. Management involvement in the diagnostic process gives them a sense of ownership of the training events that result. This encourages managers to play a positive role in the key stages pre- and post-training that do so much to reinforce, or undermine, the work of the trainer. Trainers themselves obtain better quality information on which to base training design.

Validation, Objectives and Competences

The use of the idea of 'competences' in recent training debates has brought with it some confusions, notably between competence as an individual attribute of personality (analogous to, say, extraversion) which manifests itself in all aspects of behaviour; competences as specific skills which the individual has acquired and which can be transferred from one employment or task to another; and competence as a measurable standard of performance attached to each element or task within a work role. It may be helpful to relate this to the usual three-part structure for a training objective, which allows us to make the connections shown in Figure 1.2.

TRAINING OBJECTIVE	=	JOB EQUIVALENT	=	VALIDATION EQUIVALENT
Behaviour to be performed	=	Competence (transferable skill)	=	Observable behaviour, testable skill, etc.
Standard of performance	=	Competence (measurable standard)	=	Measurement criterion
Conditions for performance	=	Workplace conditions and constraints	=	Fidelity of simulation, time, open/closed book, etc.

Figure 1.2 *Validation, objectives, and competences*

Validation within the Training Design Process

It is important to think of training as a cyclical process in which validation is just as much a key part as identification of training needs (Figure 1.3). Indeed, without validation to 'close the loop', there is no training cycle, simply a straight-line sequence from deciding upon a training activity through to implementation. With such a sequence, there is no feedback mechanism to correct errors of content or process.

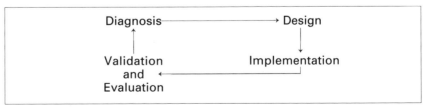

Figure 1.3 – *The training cycle (simplified model)*

Validation studies may be focused within the training event, asking 'How much has been learned?' or 'How well have the chosen methods worked?' Alternatively, validation may be focused upon workplace behaviour after the training event, when the questions are, typically, 'What improvements in performance can the trainee demonstrate?' or 'Have there been obstacles to the transfer of learning from the training event?'. Figure 1.4 illustrates the full training cycle with validation feedback loops.

The loops shown in the training cycle diagram provide feedback on the different stages, as follows:

A: Assesses the extent and impact of post-training support and/or workplace obstacles to using new knowledge and skills.

B: Assesses the quality of the training experience and the performance of the training presenters.

C: Reviews the appropriateness of the training methods to the learning objectives and to the trainees' own preferred learning styles.

D: Determines whether or not the right people have been selected for the particular training activity.

E: Measures the extent to which new knowledge or skills have been acquired; ie to what extent learning objectives have been met.

F: Examines whether the learning achieved through the training activity matches needs for competent performance of work tasks; ie to what extent are the *right* learning objectives being pursued.

The Organizational Context

We turn now to the issues involved when validation is first introduced into the organization as a part of a comprehensive training system.

Validation data can be collected in a number of ways. In some respects, the least satisfactory option, certainly in the long-term, is to hand over the whole task to an external agent, whether a consultant or academic. The impact of the validation findings is usually limited to the particular training event that is examined, and the organizational culture remains unchanged. The training department and line managers may feel little ownership of the project and rarely give much commitment to implementing changes based on its findings.

However, external specialists can provide a fast-track way into getting evaluation started. The principal benefits of using external consultants should be their expertise and impartiality, so that the validation is less likely to suffer from the bias of internal vested interests. For the smaller

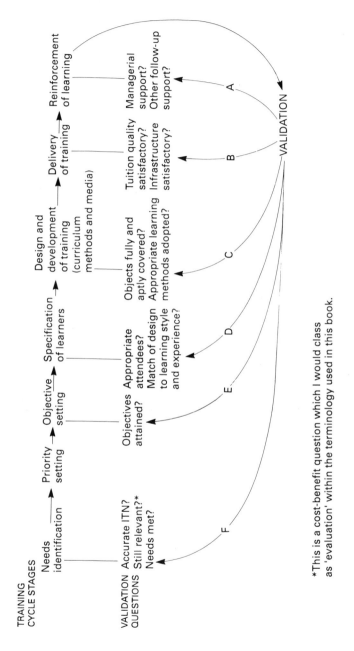

Figure 1.4 *The training cycle (extended model)*

training function, external resourcing may be the only way to get the job done. External resourcing can also be valuable in a training-of-trainers role, enabling in-house people to acquire validation skills for themselves. Success may be measured by the extent to which the client organization continues to use validation routinely over a period of time, and does not merely carry out a token validation project which then gathers dust.

Where do You Start?

Very occasionally, in large training departments, a small unit has been set up with overall responsibility for training validation and evaluation issues. More usually, the responsibility for validation falls on each individual trainer or onto sections within the training department such as course designers. The training manager may take on a quality control role, making use of a specialist consultant as expert resource and catalyst, and using the process of learning about validation as a means to enhance the skills of direct trainers and course designers.

Whichever approach is adopted, part of the validation task (particularly some elements of data collection) may be made the task of line management. Managers need support in this role, from their own trainers or from a validation unit or consultant. This support can be part of a wider process of helping managers to play a more active joint role with trainers, which helps to bridge the gap between learning and the workplace. Action planning and critical incident analysis are techniques that are especially useful to encourage management involvement.

The Politics of Measuring Training

Validation does not take place in sterile laboratory conditions, but in the arena of organizational interest groups and agendas, open and hidden. Anyone undertaking validation of training must be sensitive to these currents in organizational life. Sometimes it may be more important that a validation be seen as 'fair' than 'objective'. Sometimes validation findings will be attacked because they strike at established activities or status. By no means all of this resistance will come from trainers who perceive their favourite courses to be under attack. Managers, too, can get very defensive about pet projects, or prestige external courses that represent status symbols rather than learning opportunities.

It is naïve to pretend that validation will not identify winners and losers, good and bad in training. This sorting out of sheep and goats is especially likely to happen where the purpose of the validation is control. Typical examples are: management-commissioned reviews of training; central assessments of decentralized activities; or validation which is commissioned by the funding organization.

Every effort should be made to present validation data in a way that makes them constructive feedback on which improvements can be based, but it is generally unrealistic to assert that the training product can be evaluated without also judging the trainer or trainers responsible for it – and often the line managers who have failed to provide support before and after training, through adequate briefing, de-briefs and reinforcement. This undoubtedly accounts for much of the defensiveness among training practitioners when faced with proposals for validation.

How Much Validation do You Need?

The time you spend on validation of existing training, or developing instruments to validate future training, is time you might otherwise have spent on course development or in front of a group of trainees. It is a useful economy, therefore, to remember that not everything needs validating, nor does it need validating all the time. It is usually worth asking: 'Will the benefits of validating this piece of training justify the effort and resource costs?'

The other side of this argument is, of course, that if a training activity is not working as well as was intended, then resources are being wasted. Then, until a validation is carried out, there is no way to know with any accuracy how serious the problem is.

There are some rules of thumb for deciding amongst your priorities for validation. The criteria are:

- *Importance*: how serious would the consequences be if the training failed to work? (Incidentally, this question is also helpful in sorting out the difference between essential training and 'nice-to-know' training).
- *Frequency*: how often will the activity that you are proposing to validate take place? If the activity is one of a series, and much of the series has already run, will the validation data arrive too late to be used to modify the activity? If it is a one-off event, will the validation yield useful information that can be applied to other, different events (eg insights into the trainees' preferred methods of learning). Another way of deciding between alternative validation projects is to obtain a frequency measure from comparison of the projected trainee-hours or trainee-days for different activities.
- *Cost*: the comparison to be made here is between the costs of the training activity (and the potential loss if the training is faulty) and the

costs of carrying out a validation exercise. The wider you cast your data-collecting net, usually the greater the cost of its gathering and analysis. At the same time, bear in mind that the law of diminishing returns usually applies to the benefits from that information: more is not necessarily better quality.

● *Impact*: this is a 'political' criterion. Will this validation project trigger worthwhile changes? Will it simply be greeted with a bored 'so what's new?'. When you are first introducing validation into your organization, you do need to strike a fine balance. The riskier strategy – but the one more likely to get noticed (and, sometimes, acted upon) – is to focus validation on a high profile, allegedly 'important' or much-loved activity about which you have doubts, especially if it is one of the 'sacred cows' of current training provision. The less risky option is to pick a minor training activity serving low status staff and to produce bland and un-controversial validation findings. Mind you, nothing will change.

On balance, when first starting to use validation systematically, it makes sense to begin with a relatively modest, medium-risk project which stands a good chance of attracting cooperation and resourcing. It is then easier to build on your momentum of success when you come to tackle the more ambitious projects that are essential if validation is to fulfil its role as a catalyst of changed management and training practices.

● *Sampling*: you can use the idea of sampling (discussed in Chapter 6) to advantage in determining 'How much validation?'. You can draw up a sample based on the population of all training courses of a particular type; for example, validating 1 in 4 of your telephone skills courses. In conjunction with this, you can create a rolling programme in which each training activity is validated, over a cycle of 2 to 3 years (any longer and the validation results will probably be too late to be useful).

Designing the Validation Project

Putting the project together is fairly straightforward, provided that you deal with each of the following seven questions, summarized in Figure 1.5

1. For whom is the validation being done?
2. Which training activity is to be validated?
3. What do you want to know?
4. Who is likely to have the answers to question 3?
5. What is the appropriate technique to use?
6. When should the validation take place?
7. How will you analyse and use the data?

Figure 1.5 *Designing the validation project*

1. For Whom is the Validation being Done?

Most often, the target audience will be the trainers themselves who require feedback on what is, or is not, working in their activities. However, it is important always to ask whether other parties may have an interest in the validation findings. Managers may be concerned that training has addressed a particular performance problem; the safety officer may need to know that trained persons are capable of following proper procedures; trainees themselves may need or want feedback on their own learning progress. It certainly increases support and involvement of non-trainers in the validation process if you seek out their potential requirements before conducting the study.

You will find that many potential 'consumers' of validation studies have a very limited understanding of concepts such as validation or evaluation. They may see it as solely a matter of end-of-course reactions or 'happy data'; they may hold a simplistic cost-benefit model; or they may simply be uninformed or confused about the whole subject. You may be able to generate interest, support and understanding by running a short (half-day or one-day) workshop for managers, to get them thinking about the relevance of validation to work performance. A workshop design, based on my own in-company work, is provided in Chapter 5 (p. 93) and can be adapted to your own situation. It may come down to simply slotting a short introductory session into an existing management or supervisory event.

Formal responsibility for validation should be clear. You need to decide – and communicate – who will be responsible for design, for gathering data, for analysis and for acting on the findings. Any disagreements or ambiguities of responsibility must be resolved before going any further, otherwise they will return time and again to undermine your efforts. You also need to plan for the resourcing implications: it is unrealistic to imagine that trainers can conduct validation studies as well as maintain their existing contact hours, preparation time and so on.

2. Which Training Activity is to be Validated?

Validation cannot take place in a vacuum: you must have an actual, specific course, distance-learning pack, training exercise, or video, etc. to provide a focus for the validation. You simply cannot validate 'training in general' nor hypothetical training. The points made in the earlier section 'How much validation do you need?' are also relevant here.

Once the activity has been targeted, you should review whether the learning objectives are precise and concrete enough to stand up to validation. This is often where trainers discover that retrospective addition of validation measures to an existing piece of training can be a laborious business. Indeed, it can be quite professionally embarrassing to discover that your objectives were inadequately specified and now have to be revised. It really is an enormous saving of energy if you build validation measures into training designs from the very start of the process.

A reliable rule of thumb is this: if a person of average intelligence (who is not engaged in training or personnel work) fails to grasp from the statement of learning objectives what it is that the training is trying to achieve, then validation of that training will prove exceedingly difficult.

3. What do You Want to Know?

Earlier in this chapter, I wrote that the purpose of validation is to test the assumption that training has an effect on the work performance of trained people. The central validation question is 'Did that training make a measurable difference?'. Following this, you may want to ask 'What factors account for the training working/not working?' which focuses less on the outcome and more on the processes of design and delivery of training. Finally, you may also want to review the original needs analysis and ask, 'Were the right issues addressed by the training?'.

The questions that ask 'Did it work – and why?' may be applied within the training event or in the workplace. During a course, the trainer may wish to know 'How much has been learned?' or 'Have the learning methods worked with this kind of group?'. The answers provide information of value to trainers, and are often helpful to the trainees also. Assessments made in the workplace might ask, 'What new skills can the trained person demonstrate?' or 'What helps and what hinders the transfer of what was learnt into work practice?'.

Of course, 'Did it work?' is only shorthand; it is not a question to ask literally. In order to discover whether or not the training has achieved what was intended, you must have measures of performance before and after the training. Most of this book is devoted to describing different techniques for measuring whether different kinds of training are having an effect. These measures may be taken in the workplace or at the start and finish of a training event. Either way, the difference between the two measures is the criterion of success or failure. You can never legitimately claim improvements on the basis of just a post-training measure (which may simply reflect skills or knowledge that pre-date the training). The issue of other influences (besides the training itself) that may impinge on the measured difference pre- and post-training is discussed in the Chapter 6 section on control groups.

4. Who is Likely to Have the Answers to Question 3?

Determine who is likely to be best able to respond meaningfully to your validation questions/measures. Sometimes these people will be managers, sometimes the trainees, or third parties such as customers or colleagues. Note that this does not mean hand-picking a sample who will give you the answers you want. It does mean that you don't ask people questions that they could not reasonably be expected to answer. For example, job-transfer effects of training often can only be assessed by the learner's line manager (or, sometimes, by colleagues or subordinates). End-of-course feedback on the training event itself is better provided by the learners rather than the trainers. (It is also better if someone other than the trainers collects the end-of-course information).

Review the depth of validation you require for each targeted training activity. One may require a large sample to be assessed for skill performance, for which a behaviour observation checklist would be ideal. Another may need quite lengthy interviews with a small, focused sample. It depends on what kinds of information are required concerning which types of training.

5. What is the Appropriate Technique to Use?

Figure 1.6 enables you to cross-refer from types of training to validation techniques. A short overview of techniques is provided later in this chapter. The use of each technique is then described in full detail in Chapters 2, 3 and 4.

If you are familiar with the technique you need to use, then you can proceed with the validation design. If the technique is unfamiliar, step-by-step guidelines are provided in the next three chapters. These guides

TRAINING SUBJECT	VALIDATION TECHNIQUE
Knowledge of facts	Written test
Application of knowledge and use of procedures	Practical test Behaviour observation
Interpersonal skills	Behaviour observation Critical incident method Repertory grid
Technical (manual) skills Commercial skills	Practical tests

Figure 1.6: *Types of training subject and validation techniques*

can be employed for self-study or as the basis of a workshop for a group of trainers. (A design for an evaluation techniques workshop that has proved effective over a number of years is included in Chapter 5).

It is usually a false economy to skip a pilot implementation of the validation instrument: this enables 'bugs' to be eliminated which would otherwise undermine the value of the main application. Whenever a validation instrument is piloted, the conditions in which it is used and the kind of people with whom it is tried out must be a close approximation to what is likely to happen in the general application.

It is risky to borrow test items or questions or behaviour categories from other people's instruments. These will usually be applied to training activities which are in some degree different from the training for which the item was designed originally. Often, the amount of modification needed makes it easier to start with a clean slate.

When it comes to choosing validation techniques, there are several helpful criteria to guide you. First and most important is aptness for the purpose – the correct match between type of training and validation technique (Figure 1.6). For example, to validate technical skills training, a practical test is normally the appropriate means; to assess an interpersonal skill, some form of behaviour observation. Conversely, it would not be the most appropriate means if a written test were employed to assess interpersonal behaviour.

A second criterion is the skills available to the person conducting the validation. This is an issue of particular concern whenever validation calls for a skill that is superficially similar to, but not in fact the same as, a skill used in other kinds of personnel or training work. A frequently- encountered example of this is the unfortunate fact that the ability to conduct an effective job selection interview is not a reliable indicator of the ability to conduct a non-directive validation interview. Training of validation personnel must always be a consideration when planning projects; Chapter 5 offers guidance.

The skills issue may become an acute problem when the implementation of the validation (principally, collection of data) is delegated to people other than the validation designer, whether other trainers or line managers.

Effort must be made to 'fool-proof' the design, through pilot testing. Above all, you must take steps to ensure that the validation agents conform to instructions. There is a tendency for other people's agendas to creep into the validation process, especially where a method such as interview is used, with the result that the validation questions may be subverted or subordinated to the concerns and needs of the agent. Sometimes agents do not want to upset people to whom they defer as clients or seniors. They may steer interviews away from what they perceive to be inconvenient questions. Sometimes, agents will add questions of their own because the interview has given them access to people with whom they normally do not have contact.

Agents with poor commitment or weak understanding of the project may argue against interviewees' answers, or even tell them that they disagree with the purpose of the validation. In other instances, agents have created their own summaries of data that neither conform to the required format for further analysis, nor reflect accurately what has been said to them.

The technique needs to reflect the culture and industrial relations climate of the organization. It must be acceptable to and understandable by the subjects of the study. You need to take account of their literacy; their ability to express themselves verbally; their capacity to think intro-spectively; and whether they can think in behavioural terms. There may be occasions when an interview or verbal test has to be used, simply because of respondents' illiteracy. Sometimes, a pictorial method of conveying test information may have to be substituted for a word-based test because of language barriers.

Finally, it is sometimes worth considering secondary benefits from a particular technique. Pre-tests can act as an aid to needs analysis, as can repertory grids. Field interviewing for validation purposes sometimes carries a valuable public relations bonus for trainers who are seen to be 'getting out and about' and to be listening to feedback.

6. When should the Validation Take Place?

The timing of pre- and post-training validation is something to be re-solved case-by-case. Generally, the pre-training assessment should take place as soon as practicable before the start of training. This minimizes any effect from other sources of learning: work experience, colleagues, influences outside the organization. However, you may sometimes wish to collect a series of pre- and post-assessments over several months, to control for work-experience effects.

The timing of post-assessments is more variable. Obviously, an end-of-course test is precisely that. However, when you move validation into the workplace, the timing should be determined by how quickly you expect the trainees to put their new skills to use. That may range from immedi-ately (as, for example, with telephone skills) through to several months after training (as with some management and professional skills, which will only be evidenced if the appropriate situation arises).

If the follow-up study occurs too soon after the course, people may have had little or no opportunity to practise new skills; too late, and the course learning may have been forgotten unless it has been reinforced through regular practice. In follow-up validations, it is often worth asking about the number of times participants have had an opportunity to use what was learned, and how long an interval elapsed between the course and that use. The former has implications for who gets trained; the latter for when the training should, optimally, be given.

7. How will You Analyse and Use the Data?

Data analysis should be planned from an early stage in the project. It is frustrating to collect lots of data and then be faced with mountains of paper and no way to analyse the content. If you have suitable systems, the validation data can be directly inputted to computers for analysis; bar coding can greatly simplify this task. Guidance on data analysis and reporting validation findings is provided in Chapter 6.

Even before you know what the data signifies, it is a wise precaution to consider what actions should follow from the various conclusions that are logically possible. If there is some chance that the validation results will be negative and/or controversial, a plan for solving the identified problem will do a lot to pre-empt opposition.

It is essential that both positive and critical validation findings lead to action – and are seen to do so. Nothing contributes more to cynicism about validation than a perception that it is a cosmetic exercise which collects data which then merely gather dust in the bottom of the trainer's filing cabinet.

Techniques Overview

Chapters 2, 3 and 4 describe in detail how you can use each of the main validation techniques. What follows here is a brief overview of those techniques.

1. Interview

Interview is the ideal method where explanation of actions and decisions is needed, where you need to explore subjects' thought processes, or where the kinds of answer you get are likely to be open-ended.

The interview should be based upon a prepared schedule of open-ended questions, and typically permits ad hoc follow-up questions to explore responses in more depth or to clarify what the respondent has said. Interviews are usually recorded by the interviewer either in writing or on tape. It should be noted that the interview itself and subsequent data analysis are very time-consuming. As a rule, therefore, the technique is limited to small numbers of subjects.

Interviews are usually conducted one-to-one by a trained interviewer, mostly face-to-face though occasionally by telephone.The length of an interview may range from a few minutes up to about an hour, although 30–40 minutes maximum is a good rule-of-thumb for interviewers who do not want to outstay their welcome.

2. Critical Incident Review

This self-report technique asks subjects to complete a regular diary of 'critical incidents' for subsequent analysis. The diary records their direct observations of their own workplace behaviour at moments throughout the day that they consider to be significant ('critical') in the performance of their job roles.

Typical applications are where validation data concerning subordinates need to be obtained from supervisory management, or where direct observation of trained persons would be unreasonably intrusive. When used properly, the strength of the technique is that it puts behavioural reality into good-natured but empty assertions such as 'That was a fantastic course!' or 'That training totally altered the whole way I think about the job'.

How long the diary needs to be maintained will depend on the nature of the job, ie, upon how frequently 'critical incidents' occur. The data are examined by the person conducting the validation for evidence of any connections between the training objectives (and content) and observable job behaviours described in the diary.

3. Repertory Grid

This technique identifies the behaviours that subjects perceive as correlates of effective and ineffective performance. The technique is complicated, time-consuming and occasionally provokes hostility from subjects who have difficulty making the conceptual insights that it requires. However, it can give interesting results not readily available by other means. Where it is used as a diagnostic element in training, especially for personal development, it is the logical method to employ for subsequent assessment of learning gain and changes in perception.

Note that it does not measure actual changes in how people work, just changes in their perceptions of a given subject (which may reflect serious misunderstandings). Nor does the method provide a reliable predictor of performance improvements, given the unpredictable linkage between attitude change and behaviour.

4. Written Test

These tests assess changes in factual knowledge (including knowledge – but not use – of procedures). Whenever skills have to be tested, written tests can only be a poor substitute for practical testing or behaviour observation methods. Nevertheless, written tests do provide an objective measure of whether trainees can restate what they have been taught.

Tests can easily be administered to large groups of trainees. They are relatively low cost to develop and implement, and they do yield precise validation data if used properly.

5. Practical Test

This is the appropriate validation technique wherever trainees must translate knowledge into application. Practical tests may focus upon the finished task or upon the process of performance. A single task may be assessed, or a sequence of tasks forming a procedure.

A well-designed test will yield reliable, quantifiable validation data. The cost of practical testing varies widely, being greatest where test equipment needs to be constructed to simulate the operations and faults of machinery.

6. Behaviour Observation

Behaviour observation is of course a type of practical test, in which the person trained in some aspect of interpersonal skills (as distinct from the technical or commercial skills which are the focus of practical tests) demonstrates the ability to perform that skill.

The technique provides a method for accurate, systematic observation of verbal and physical behaviour before, during and after training. Post-training assessment in the workplace is often the most useful application, although this usually depends on the involvement of managers or supervisors. Behaviour observation instruments require very careful preparation, plus the training of observers. Data analysis itself is a comparatively simple process.

The strength of the technique is that it emphasizes observable behaviour and discourages guessing at subjects' attitudes. This gives it its objectivity, as well as acting as a reinforcement of behavioural learning objectives.

2 Testing Knowledge

┌───┐

▷   SUMMARY   ◁

- Where training is concerned to impart knowledge, written tests offer an effective
  and economical technique for validation. This chapter summarizes the applications of such tests as well as their limitations. Resistance to testing is discussed. The
  chapter then describes the eight general stages for putting together effective tests.
  The use of open- and closed- book tests is also discussed.
- Further sections describe in detail the particular features of the different kinds of
  tests of knowledge, as well as the design considerations attaching specifically to
  each one. The techniques covered are: recall items (sentence completion, short-
  answer and essay); and recognition items (multiple-choice question, true/false
  choice and list-matching). .

└───┘

Applications

Tests of knowledge should be applied only to training where the ability to
remember and restate facts – individual facts, facts in groups, or facts in
procedural sequences – is the essential element in the learning process.
In practice, this applies to a much narrower range of learning activities
than might be expected; most organizational training focuses upon the
application of facts rather than upon knowledge pure and simple.

Sometimes, organizational pressures require written tests to be used
where either practical tests or behaviour observation methods would be
more thorough. In any situation where the learning would be assessed

more realistically by watching the trainee do the task rather than write about it, the use of a pencil-and-paper test will be second-best. Sometimes, it may be dangerously inadequate. For example, it is one thing to ask a learner driver; 'Describe what you would do to turn right at a roundabout'; and another for the learner to coordinate eyes, hands and feet to control gears, acceleration and steering whilst finding a gap in busy traffic. However, when following a 'part-whole' training model, it may be quite acceptable to use knowledge tests as a check on the intermediate parts of the learning, with a performance test for the completed whole.

The main applications for tests of knowledge are:

- Pre-training: as a diagnostic instrument to determine the level of existing knowledge amongst trainees, in order to define the baseline of knowledge deficiency from which learning objectives can be set.
- During training: to provide an assessment of progress – mainly of benefit as corrective feedback to the trainees themselves.
- Before and after training: as a measure of the amount of learning that has occurred overall – informing trainers about whether or not knowledge has been absorbed and hence whether or not the training methods have been effective
- At the start of training: as a trigger to debate about the proposed learning goals.
- Following training: first, as a certification of competence (proof that the trainees have the necessary knowledge, but not, of course, proof that they have acquired that knowledge through the training activity); second, as reinforcement, through repetition, of what has been learned.

Resistance to Testing

The objection is sometimes raised that learners resent tests, associating them with negative memories of their school days. Much depends upon the climate within the organization and the quality of the relationships between managers, trainees and trainers. Trainees are usually quite interested to know how well they are doing and tests provide a more objective assessment of progress than any other method. It helps if tests are seen as a useful part of quality control within the organization's training activities and as a source of information that will be helpful to the trainees themselves.

On the other hand, if tests are regarded as mainly punitive in intent, then naturally there will be caution and resistance to their use. Similarly, if tests are used to rank groups of employees, the training aspects will be perceived to be secondary to the performance assessment aspects, and resistance can be expected. (When comparing scores within a group, the use of gain ratios – the amount each person has learned, relative to his or her starting point – is preferable to the use of raw scores.)

Resistance to tests can sometimes be traced to the poor design of the test itself. If there is a bias in the choice of items to be tested or in the wording of questions, or if the test addresses only trivial aspects of the topic, then the test will lack credibility. A good test assesses knowledge of all important aspects of the subject and that knowledge should relate directly to the learning objectives and to the job tasks that underpin the objectives.

Types of Test Item

There are two types of test item: 'recall' (also called 'supply') and 'recognition'. In the case of recall items, the trainee must recall from memory the answer to the test question. Recognition items prompt the trainee with a number of alternative possible answers.

Recall items may require a single-word answer (sometimes as a word that completes a sentence), a short descriptive paragraph or an essay. Recognition items include multiple-choice questions, true/false choices and verbal or visual list-matching questions. Both recall and recognition items may be included within the same test – the choice of item type is determined by the subject matter to be tested.

Tests using either type of item may be run as 'open book' or 'closed book' tests. Sometimes it is important that trainees carry information in their heads and a closed-book test without access to any reference material will be appropriate. In other situations, the job task requires people to be able to find their way around reference sources (eg, technical manuals, procedural interpretations of statutes, codes of practice) which are available to them at work. In the latter case, an open-book test is appropriate and the reference source material should be available to the trainees during the test.

Designing Tests – The Stages

Stage 1

Choose all the elements of the training that you want to test. Be selective – only include the more important topics. The challenge is to balance the development of a valid test that adequately covers the subject matter against, first, the resourcing costs and, second, the risk that a short test will be unrepresentative of the whole. There is also the need to avoid the trap of selecting test topics because they are easy to measure rather than because they are significant subjects. Measuring trivia devalues testing. Limit the test items to what has been presented during the training activity.

Stage 2

Check out the quality of the learning objectives to be tested. Weak objectives make for imprecise tests. Ensure that objectives comply with the three-part design of 'Observable Behaviour-Conditions for Performance-Standard Required'. If necessary, redraft the learning objectives before attempting test design.

Stage 3

Match the types of test item you will use to the subject matter to be tested: is recall the issue, or recognition? Is a more complex procedural chain involved? Will it be an open- or closed-book test? All the various kinds of recall and recognition items may be included within the same test and this can provide some useful variety.

Stage 4

Draft a number of test items for each learning objective that you are assessing. The aim should be to create a test bank of items that allows you to select a different mix of questions each time you use the test. This greatly reduces the scope for cheating. It also allows you to discard any items that prove to be weak discriminators between good and poor trainees.

It is essential that all items within each test sub-group in the bank present equal difficulty to the trainee. Otherwise, the test as a whole will be more or less difficult on different occasions, depending upon which items are included, and it will not then be possible to make valid comparisons between one training event and another.

Some general rules for design of test items follow. Guidance specific to particular types of item appears in the later sections where examples of each type are given:

● Questions should not contain clues to the answer. This is most obvious with leading questions; it is also a matter of whether some alternatives provided are more plausible than others. More subtly, a question may give clues to the answer to another question within the same test. Exclude any question which could be easily answered by someone who had not undergone the training.

● All tests using written language (ie, not purely visual and/or verbally administered) presume a level of literacy: test designers need to take care that a test does not require a higher level of literacy than is needed for competence in the job that trainees perform. More generally, there is no advantage to be gained from making the wording of questions deliberately obscure (unless this obscurity accurately mirrors conditions in the workplace!). Aim for plain, clear language. Validation should not become a test of the trainees' ability to unravel complex syntax. Lastly, avoid trick wordings and items phrased as negative questions. You are setting out to test trainees' knowledge, not to test their ability to take tests.

● Wherever possible, paraphrase rather than quote directly words and phrases used in the training sessions. Where possible, place the knowledge under test in a different context to that used during the training itself. {This will provide a better test of whether the trainee has assimilated the meanings behind the words, rather than merely the ability to parrot the 'right' answer.

● Avoid conscious or accidental patterns in recognition items. Do not, for example, always make the correct answer in a four-option multiple-choice question option number three. Sequences of true/false items sometimes form unintended repeating patterns (eg,true-true-false-true-true-false). With true/false and multiple-choice items, use a dice to randomly determine the position of the correct answer.

● When designing test items, have as your aim the development of items for each of which there is only one correct answer. This will not usually apply to extended essay items, but for all other test items there should be no ambiguity or choice concerning the correct answer.

● Do not link questions in such a way that the ability to answer one question depends upon getting a previous question right.

Stage 5

Put the test items into a sequence that makes sense to trainees – most commonly, the order in which the elements of knowledge would be used in work tasks. Plan the layout of the test document. Decide whether trainees will write their answers on the test document or on a separate answer document. Where appropriate, make provision for computerized marking of answers.

With a test bank on a word processor, it is a simple matter to 'cut-and-paste' each selection of questions into the correct sequence. However, it is essential that clear instructions are laid down by the test designer so that subsequent assemblers of test item selections will know which sub-groups of item must be represented and by how many items.

Stage 6

Draft instructions to the test subjects. Tell them simply and clearly what they have to do during the test (eg, tick boxes). Make sure that the instructions appear at the start of the test. Where there is a variety of responses to items (ticks, crosses, cross out alternatives, write in words, circle options, etc.) it is essential that the appropriate instruction is repeated against every item or against every group of items of a particular, identical kind (eg, if all the true/false items are grouped together).

Stage 7

Draft the scoring key for marking the results of the test. Where tests are marked manually (rather than with OCR or bar-code computer systems) design the key so that it can be overlaid on the test answer document.

The most important principle in scoring is consistency: the same test paper marked by different assessors using the scoring key correctly should yield identical scores. A well-designed scoring key removes all (or virtually all) discretion from the marking process and again success lies in having well-defined learning objectives to begin with.

Stage 8

Pre-testing is always essential to debug the test bank. Questions that the designer believes to be crystal-clear may have ambiguous meanings for test subjects. Test items may show up differences between good and bad trainees. Different test items on the same subject matter may vary in difficulty. In multinational or multicultural contexts, tests may contain unnoticed cultural bias or assumptions that are not equally valid for all test subjects.

Run the test a number of times with trainees similar or identical to the target population. If possible, discuss perceptions of the test with each person after the trial run. Apply statistical assessments to the test – the index of discrimination, facility value, test-retest correlation (Chapter 5). Then revise test items, test instructions and layout and the scoring key as necessary.

Recall (Supply) Items – Completion Items

These consist of 1) an unfinished statement requiring a word or short phrase to complete it, 2) a statement with one or two significant words omitted, or 3) a presentation of information from which the answer may be deduced, eg, a graph

---

EXAMPLES

1) The meaning of a traffic light when it shows an amber light is.......... .

2) A training objective comprises three elements – the..........., the conditions under which it will be performed, and the ....

3) From the graph, find the value of X when Y = 6

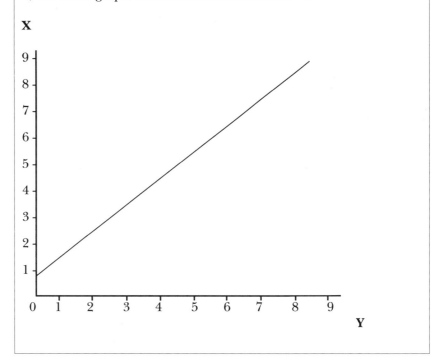

Additional Guidelines for Completion Items

- An omitted word should be placed towards the end, rather than the beginning, of a sentence.
- As a rule, do not omit more than two key words in one sentence.
- The omitted words must be directly and significantly related to the learning objective.
- There should only be one way to complete the sentence that makes sense.
- It is very easy for completion items to degenerate into trivia and for the answers to be obvious even to non-trained persons.

Recall (Supply) Items – Essay

Essay questions are easily set but less easily assessed in any consistent manner. They do permit tests of broader groupings of knowledge than the isolated fact, for example descriptions of formal procedures or diagnostic sequences. Essay is the preferred method where the trainee's ability to argue logically, analyse, explain or compare is the central task.

EXAMPLE

Describe the organizational factors which influence the extent that training leads to changes in performance at work.

Although an essay should not become a test of the Eng.Lit. skills of the trainee, it does tend to give an advantage to the person who knows less but can write more fluently than other trainees. Whenever possible, break essay-type questions down into a number of short-answer items which will provide both quicker testing and easier, more objective marking.

Essay is a time-consuming technique for both trainee and for assessor. Marking usually results in more subjective assessments than other test methods and may depend upon there being a subject matter expert available to assess and interpret the essay answers consistently across the trainee group. A marking key should be developed which specifies the various matters for which subjects will gain marks: coverage of content, logical structuring of arguments, validity of analysis, clarity of communication. Marking consistency is improved if the marker works through all trainees' responses to a single essay question before moving on to the next one; it is good practice to have an independent assessor to re-mark a proportion of the essay answers.

Recall (Supply) Items – Short Answer

Short-answer items typically require answers that are one or two sentences in length; summarized or tabulated answers are usually preferable to continuous prose. Examples of short-answer items would include lists, brief descriptions of rules, statements of situational factors and stages in an activity sequence. Both short-answer and essay questions should give trainees clear guidance on the target length of their answers.

EXAMPLE

Describe (in not more than 50 words) what is meant by the 'Index of Discrimination' in validation of tests.

Summarize the three main elements that make up a well-drafted training objective.

What does each of the following initials stand for?

ISE...

IFA...

E&OE...

FIMBRA...

When the marking key is drawn up, the test designer must recognize that there are likely to be valid answers additional to the ones they have thought of themselves. Over a period of use, the key will gradually expand to include virtually all acceptable responses.

Recognition Items – Multiple-Choice Questions

Multiple-choice questions are useful where the training objective requires that the learner recognize, differentiate or describe factual elements. A question with four or five equally plausible answers makes it much harder to guess the answer correctly (25 or 20 per cent chance). Unlike true/false questions, the correct answer does not have to be absolutely and invariably the case; it must just be a significantly better choice than the other options (which are known as 'distractors'). Indeed, all the options may be correct, with the trainee's judgement being tested in deciding which is most appropriate in response to the question.

Multiple-choice items are quickly administered and easily {and objectively marked. Their construction does, however, require some effort. Some rules for drafting follow:

- The 'stem' is a question or statement, from which all the answers must follow both in terms of subject relevance and grammar. Where the stem is a descriptive statement, it need not be restricted to a single sentence.
- Four or five options for the correct answer are desirable; it is more important, though, to have distractors that are plausible and it is bad practice to make up the number with general phrases such as 'all of the above'; to the person who does not know the correct answer, all of the options should appear equally likely.
- The answer options may be single words, sentences, images, numbers or letters keyed to some other material, mathematical products.
- Beware of unintended cues which give away the correct answer: a common failing is to make it more specific and detailed, or stating a different viewpoint to the distractors; avoid ending the stem with the indefinite article or mixing singular and plural nouns between stem and distractors.
- Avoid making distractors synonyms of each other, or having them overlap conceptually; do not repeat in the distractors any distinctive word or phrase that appears in the stem.

EXAMPLE

When a person is preparing for a new job role, the most appropriate training method to use is:

action learning

sensitivity training   (tick one)

role play

group discussion

Recognition Items – True/False Questions

These two-option questions take the form of a statement followed either by true/false or agree/disagree. There is always a 50 per cent chance of guessing the correct option. True/false questions in effect ask: 'Is this statement wholly true or wholly false?'. They are unsuited to controversial topics or to any statement that admits to shades of grey.

Additional Guidelines for Designing True/False Questions

– Avoid complicated statements. If a long statement is unavoidable, break it down into short sentences.
– Never have more than one idea in the question statement. Otherwise, the trainee may wish to answer 'true' to one element and 'false' to another in the question.
– Bear in mind that few statements are always true or always false. Adjectives and adverbs that refer to absolutes: 'all', 'every', 'never', 'always' are warnings that the statement probably has got some exceptions to it somewhere – which the trainee will probably pick up on.
– Aim for roughly equal numbers of 'true' and 'false' correct answers and randomize the order in which they occur within the test.

Recognition Items – Matching Items

This method utilizes two sets of elements and requires the trainee to pair items in one list with items in the other. The sets of elements may comprise words, graphics or numbers, or a mixture of these elements. Matching-item tests are comparatively easy to put together and are easily scored. They are effective in testing selection or recognition of knowledge elements and the unequal lengths of the matched lists makes guessing difficult.

EXAMPLE

1) Matching items (word lists)

Draw a pencil line linking the training writers named in the left-hand column with the concepts listed in the right-hand column.

Schein	Behavioural objectives
McGregor	Achievement motivation
Argyris	Career anchors
Mager	Anticipatory socialization
McClelland	Confrontation meeting
	Double-loop learning
	Theory X and Y managers
	Management by objectives.

---

2) Matching items (word list plus graphics)

Match numbered items on the machine to the descriptions in the left hand column:

Insert correct
numbers below

a. Upper register .....

b. Shift lever .....

c. Main crank handle .....

d Lower register .....

e. Register clearing handle .....

f. Keyboard .....

g. Tabulator .....

h. Subtraction lever .....

g. Water inlet .....

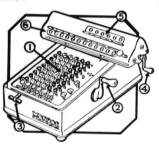

FIG. 62. THE MONROE CALCULATING
MACHINE

Additional Guidelines for Constructing Matched-Item Lists

- The list of items to be matched (left-hand list) should be kept within the range 5–10 items, with about one-and-a-half times as many items in the right-hand list from which the trainee must choose.
- All items in the lists must relate to the same learning topic and all the items in the right-hand list must be plausible alternatives.
- To speed up the test process for trainees, place items in a logical order – alphabetical, numerical, chronological, etc.
- Both lists must appear on the same page.
- It is particularly important that the instructions are clear on what action the trainee should take, eg, to draw lines linking items or to write down the matching pairs, etc.

3 Testing Interpersonal Skills

▷ SUMMARY ◁

- There are three parts to this chapter, each concerned with a different approach to the validation of interpersonal skills training. The first section describes how you can develop behaviour observation instruments; the second covers self-report techniques (critical incident method and interview); and the third section shows you how to use a repertory grid to obtain behavioural data that reflect changes in attitude following training.

Introduction

Interpersonal skills training is one of the least simple areas to validate, but one in which the rewards for adopting a more rigorous approach greatly outweigh the effort. The core task when validating interpersonal skills training is to obtain concrete evidence that training has changed *behaviour*. Hence, the less the validation depends upon self-report methods or upon assessments of attitude, and the more that it depends upon observation of trainees' performance by trained observers, using purpose-designed validation instruments, the better the quality of information and the more effective the reinforcement of learning. This chapter will cover self-report methods and one technique for assessing attitude change, but the main focus will be upon methods for systematically observing behaviour.

The range of activities encompassed by the term 'interpersonal skills' is broad: from team-work in the boardroom to telephone use on the reception desk, supervisory and management skills, selling skills, counselling, decision-making, non-racist and non-sexist behaviour, chairing meetings, training and coaching, customer service and so on. Interpersonal skills concern the ways in which people act towards each other, verbally and non-verbally. Attitudes and personal constructs are at best a predisposition to act in a certain way and it is the case that people act in ways that conflict with their expressed attitudes or, conversely, hold attitudes which they do not translate into actions. Attitudes may be inferred but behaviour can be observed, shaped and developed, by trainers and managers.

The validation techniques that will be discussed here may be applied to interpersonal skills training at a number of points in the cycle:

- as a preliminary assessment, part of needs analysis and/or the identification of individual learning needs within a course structure;
- as a pre/post-activity measure of changes in behaviour attributable to training using either on-course or workplace measurement;
- as on-course feedback and learning reinforcement for trainees (as when the validation instrument is used as an adjunct to role plays);
- as an end-of-training certification of competence.

There are three elements of interpersonal behaviour that validation studies may focus on:

- the content of the behavioural transaction: analysing what kinds of behaviour could be observed (eg, helpful or obstructive behaviours);
- the achievement of the task: analysing how effectively a specified task requiring use of interpersonal skills was carried out (eg, did people learn from the presentation? did the group reach a 'good' decision?);
- the qualities of the behaviours demonstrated (analysing each of the behaviours in terms of its duration, frequency, sequence and quality).

Behaviour Observation Instruments

At its simplest, it may be enough for the trainer to know whether or not a particular behaviour was exhibited at all. It may be desirable to know the frequency with which different kinds of behaviour were exhibited and this may be correlated with different individuals within a group and/or with different time periods within the whole observation. Alternatively, the focus may be upon the frequencies with which individuals contribute, or upon the patterns of who interacts with whom. The focus of validation may be shifted from the people performing the skills to those on the receiving end, using validation instruments designed to measure the effects of the performance.

The analysis of behaviour content may be made on the basis of either time sampling or unit sampling. With time sampling, a series of observation times are defined, according to the nature of the activity to be observed. The time intervals may be as frequent as every 30 seconds or as intermittent as hourly. In unit sampling, the observer records every instance when each category of specified behaviour occurs. Although time sampling is more economical, the trainer is usually interested in all occurrences of specified behaviours and will therefore employ unit sampling.

A third distinction is that between validation instruments which can be used to analyse the behaviour of several people within a group interaction (eg, a discussion meeting) and those which focus upon an individual. The latter may be interacting with another individual (eg, in a sales situation) or with a group (eg, a manager presenting a report to the board).

Observation Paranoia

Probably the most frequent concern that I hear during the validation workshops I run for trainers is that the trainees' awareness of being watched will invalidate any conclusions drawn by the observer. To this may be added an additional concern about the 'unreal' nature of role play exercises. Both concerns are understandable but, I would suggest, generally over-stated, especially when an analogy is claimed to Heisenberg's uncertainty principle.

Of course role plays tend to make people more self-conscious but many people not only learn skills through this method, but find value in the feedback which they get from tutors and their peer group. The very fact of participating in interpersonal skills training is likely to make the participants more accustomed to looking at their own and other's behaviour in a structured and appraising manner.

When observation takes place in the workplace, the process may retain its formal structure but be less intrusive. It is ethically desirable that subjects know that they may be subjected to an assessment by observation of their workplace behaviour, but the actual observation may well take place without their awareness. After all, most managers regularly observe informally what their staff are doing. Salespeople have long been accustomed to getting feedback from their managers at 'kerbside conferences' after a client visit. Often the individual's career progress may depend on casual and subjective assessments whereas properly-designed validation instruments put such assessments on a much more rational footing.

Methods of Observation

There are three possibilities: direct observation (of role play or in the workplace); indirect observation using a video recording of role-played or 'live' behaviours; and indirect observation using a sound recording.

Indirect observations have the advantage that they allow action replays of complex incidents which might be difficult to track live. They make it possible for different observers to independently analyse the material as a cross-check on data-coding reliability. Sound recording is also the most realistic way of observing interpersonal skills on the telephone, where visual cues may distract an observer.

On the debit side, indirect methods increase the cost of validation because the analysis takes longer than live observation (as a rule of thumb, double the time). A video camera and prowling operator is probably more intrusive than a seated observer with clipboard, and it is usually difficult to keep all members of a group activity in frame.

Direct observation is least time-consuming and has the added value that it allows almost instant feedback to trainees. Where complex behaviours are to be validated, direct observation calls for thoroughly-trained observers; group activities often require several observers. The more trainees involved, the higher the activity rate and the larger the number of behaviours to be tracked, the greater the number of observers required. As a guideline, one trained observer should manage to track 3–5 trainees displaying 6–8 categories of behaviour.

The more complex the behaviours to be tracked, the more important it becomes that observers receive planned training in the use of observation instruments. The categories of behaviour on a validation instrument must mean the same to each and every observer. Some suggestions for training of observers are made in Chapter 5. The observers themselves may be drawn from amongst training staff or from line management. Peer group observers are very useful for more informal behaviour observation within training courses. Involving managers in training is desirable but experience suggests that there is a common tendency to judge trainees on the basis of whether or not they would fit into the manager's own unit, rather than on whether or not the specified behaviours have been exhibited. Training managers for the observer role is particularly necessary.

Designing the Observation Instrument

There is no universal checklist suitable for all instances of behaviour observation. The categories of behaviour to be included in the instrument must always be derived from the learning objectives of the training to be validated. When you start to design any validation instrument, it is helpful to make a list of the learning objectives that you are validating. You can then more easily track the linkage between observation categories, test items, etc, and the elements of training which these are intended to measure.

Most behaviour observation instruments consist of a two-way matrix, with behaviour categories along one side and analysis columns along the other. At its simplest, the analysis columns may be labelled for frequency of occurrence. A more detailed analysis measures frequency within the time periods during the observation, or frequency by individuals within a group. Other designs allow (or require) the observer to write in comments and examples of the behaviours under observation. A number of illustrations appear in Figures 3.1–3.5.

BEHAVIOUR CATEGORIES	FREQUENCY OF OCCURRENCE
Listening	~~///~~ ~~///~~ ////
Giving information	~~///~~ //// ~~///~~
Making proposals	~~///~~ ~~///~~ //// ~~///~~
Arguing against others' proposals	~~///~~ //

Figure 3.1 *Simple frequency analysis*

BEHAVIOUR CATEGORIES	FREQUENCY OF OCCURRENCE (PER 15 MINUTE OBSERVATION PERIODS)			
	0-15	16-30	31-45	46-60
Listening	//	////	/	///
Giving information	#### ///	///	//	////
Making proposals	#### ////	####	///	// //
Arguing against others' proposals	//	///	////	#### //

Figure 3.2 *Frequency analysis within time periods*

The matrices in Figures 3.1 and 3.2 may be used for observation of one person's behaviour, or to validate changes in the behaviour of a group of trainees. The matrix in Figure 3.3 is used for observation of each person's behaviour within a group interaction. The number of columns for trainees can be extended – the only limitation is the observer's ability to track behaviour accurately. In some instances, it may be more appropriate to use role titles in place of names.

	TRAINEES			
BEHAVIOURS	Zoe	David	Minette	Caroline
Listening	#### ####	////	/ ####	///
Giving information	////	// ####	/	///
Making proposals	//	////	///	/
Arguing against others' proposals	//	//// ####	//// ####	/
Supporting and building upon others' proposals	///	/	/	///

Figure 3.3 *Frequency analysis with named participants*

Where the particular element of the training is concerned with not only quantity of contributions, but also with who speaks to whom, the matrix in Figure 3.4 provides a practical means for tracking this. As with the previous example, it may sometimes be more appropriate to use role titles in place of names.

RECEIVERS	SENDERS				
	Zoe	David	Minette	Caroline	Totals (sent)
Zoe		////	/ ###	///	13
David	///		/	///	7
Minette	//	////		/	7
Caroline	/	//// ###	//// ###		19
Totals (received)	6	17	16	7	46

Figure 3.4 *Frequency analysis of named participants' interactions*

The checklist in Figure 3.5 is useful as a first stage instrument where a number of behaviour categories (defined from learning objectives) require validation. The observer writes in relevant examples of the behaviours as they occur, including bad as well as good instances. Write-in observations of this kind provide a basis for more formalized checklists such as the one shown in Figure 3.6. This type of open-ended observation is often helpful when trying to validate rather fuzzy training objectives such as those which use phrases like 'appropriate', 'constructively' or 'well'.

Selecting Categories for Behaviour Observation Validation Instruments

Step 1
Develop the categories from behaviourally-stated learning objectives which, in turn, reflect the job tasks for which training is being provided. As part of the validation process, it should be possible to distinguish trained from untrained persons in the workplace, solely on the basis of observations structured by the instrument.

Observable behaviours are not the same as personality traits. 'Smiles' is a description of what the observer can see; 'pleasant personality', on the other hand, is a subjective inference which is not readily verifiable. Validation is concerned with the observable outcomes of training, not with intuitions and still less with wishful thinking.

TELEPHONE USE TRAINING VALIDATION	Observer:	Trainee: Date:
Behaviour drawn from learning objectives	Is the behaviour present? Y/N?	Brief description of the behaviour observed. Comments on the quality of performance
Greets caller		
Establishes the purpose of the call		
Chooses appropriate language		
Uses courteous tone of voice		
Handles complaints constructively		
Provides information that customer needs		
Closes call well		

Figure 3.5 *Simple 'write-in' instrument*

Step 2

Selectivity is usually necessary: focus observation on the more important behaviours – importance being determined by how critical that behaviour is to the success or failure of the activity in question. Always examine negative as well as positive behaviours. An observer will have difficulty tracking more than five or six types of behaviour within a group of about six people, although the skill grows with training and practice. A large group will always need several observers – in very active situations, shadowing participants one-to-one.

Step 3

Determine the right level of emphasis for selected categories. This is a matter of context. For example, validation of listening skills training will require close attention to the many elements of listening, whereas validation of, say, management training may include 'listening skills' as a single category amongst others.

Step 4

Each category must be conceptually distinct. If there is overlap or ambiguity about where the boundary lies, then different observers will interpret the behaviour categories in different ways and consistency will be lost. This problem is increased, the fuzzier the behavioural descriptions that are being used, eg, 'unsuitable response', 'poor attitude'.

Step 5

Prepare a description of actions, words and phrases to be used, examples of body language, procedural details and so on to encapsulate fully each behavioural category. Describe the categories in plain English which trainer, trainee and observer will all understand in the same way. These descriptions should include both negative and positive examples. The descriptions that would be written in by an observer (eg, using the matrix in Figure 3.5) often provide the quickest – though not always the most comprehensive – listing. The example in Figure 3.6 shows how that matrix might develop into a structured checklist.

Step 6

Organize the behaviour categories into a logical order – usually, the sequence in which they are most likely to occur during the observation period. Where behaviours recur during the observation period, it may make more sense (to observers) if those behaviours are grouped by type of activity rather than order of occurrence.

Step 7

Try out the observation instrument on a representative group of people.

TELEPHONE USE TRAINING VALIDATION	Observer:	Trainee:	Date:
Behaviour categories	**Examples of Relevant Behaviour** (circle instances observed)		
	POSITIVE EXAMPLES	NEGATIVE EXAMPLES	
Greets caller	Uses caller's surname. Identifies self. Uses good morning (etc).	Omits caller's/own name. Uses caller's first name.	
Establishes the purpose of the call	Asks open and probing questions. Gives verbal summary of purpose.	No clear purpose. Waffles. Fails to gather information needed. No summary.	
Chooses appropriate language	No jargon, company abbreviations, or technical terms. Does not talk down.	Confusing use of jargon etc. Use of emotive words. Patronising tone.	
Uses courteous tone of voice	Clear. Interesting tone. Varies pace. Conveys warmth.	Mumbles. Monotonous tone. Speaks too fast. Sounds coldly bureaucratic. Aggressive.	
Handles complaints constructively	Listens carefully. Gives summary. Involves customer in solution. Proposes actions.	Becomes defensive/aggressive. Argues the facts. No solution proposed.	
Provides information that customer needs	Checks need. Gives information clearly. Is accurate. Clarifies if necessary.	Misunderstands need. Inaccurate. Unclear. Ignores/mishandles questions.	
Closes call well	Thanks caller. Summarizes conversation.	Abrupt close. No summary of action.	

Figure 3.6 Behaviour observation instrument.

At this stage, much can be learned by allowing *un*trained observers to use the instrument; this is a quick way to reveal any flaws. It also helps your preparations for formal training of observers.

Step 8

Train the observers. Chapter 5 provides guidance on organizing and delivering such training.

Step 9

Using the data. Behaviour observation data show whether or not people can perform the skills which the training has tried to impart. A pre-training observation, as well as one post-training, is essential if you want to link learning gain to the training activity. Ideally, a number of observations should be collected over a period in order to give a more representative sampling of behaviour.

The data relating to an individual can also be used for personal feedback. This should concentrate on describing the person's behaviours, positive and negative, and should avoid making comparisons with other individuals – nor should some notional overall rating of that individual be offered. The purpose of feedback is to improve performance, so always focus on the behavioural details so that the person knows exactly what needs to be changed.

In a validation application, individual data may either be analysed to show the changes in the pattern of behaviour pre/post (see Chapter 6 on statistical methods) or may be consolidated, using a master observation sheet, to provide a single pre/post comparison for the whole trainee group.

Self-report Methods

All techniques for validation which rely on self-report by the trainees will inevitably run the risk that the data might be biased, distorted, partial or simply mistaken (eg, the subject believes that behaviour has been assertive, whereas colleagues perhaps see it as aggressive). There is the additional risk that interpretation of the data by the validator may introduce additional elements of subjectivity. That said, self- reported data may be all that you can sometimes obtain.

Direct observation may be impractical because of its impact on third parties (most typically where clients would be part of the observed interaction and confidentiality is an issue). Observation may also be ruled out because of the impracticality of continuous shadowing of trainees in situations where the target behaviours occur intermittently and unpredictably over a long period of time. Typical applications of the technique have included validation of training for supervisors, for advice workers and for fraud investigators. In such circumstances, self-report validation is likely to be the best that can be achieved. Two forms of self-report are described here: the critical incident diary; and interview.

Critical Incident Diaries

As with other techniques, critical incident offers multiple applications: needs identification, reinforcement of learning and validation.

The core of the method is the collection of examples of workplace behaviour that have particular significance for the job role under scrutiny – hence they are incidents that are 'critical' to success or failure. This method has been found to have high face-validity with users, who report that it addresses the realities of their work and allows them to communicate their own understanding of problems and how they are handled. The great strength of the technique is that it uses behaviourally-defined criteria of effective performance in job settings.

The validation process consists of making comparisons of the frequency and type of incident and the ways in which incidents were handled before and after training. An example of the use of critical incident diaries would be following, say, time management training, to log interruptions by subordinates and telephone calls and to analyse how these were dealt with.

Critical incident data can, in principle, be collected by observers (managers, colleagues, subordinates or training staff), although it then simply becomes a variation on behaviour observation, but it is more usual for data to be recorded by the person who has undergone the training. The data are collected in a critical incident diary which provides a structure for capturing the essential points in the interaction.

The timing of data collection is a further issue: an immediate record following the incident may be better at capturing feelings from the moment; an end-of-day record may be more considered and often fits better into work schedules. The number of incidents to be recorded is also a factor. If there is likely to be more than a couple of relevant incidents to record in a working day, details may become confused if making the record is delayed.

The kind of information to be collected must be made clear. The requirement is to record actual events and behaviour. This may include introspection regarding the diary subject's own thought processes and emotions but it must exclude inferences about other people's state of mind. It also excludes statements about hypothetical situations. The more the data are specific and grounded in factual examples, the greater their credibility. Again, use of a standard diary format for each incident is helpful.

The format may include some data categories that are specific to a particular activity, but as a general layout the example in Figure 3.7 will have quite wide applications.

CRITICAL INCIDENT DIARY   Date:.........   Sheet No.........

Please complete one diary sheet for each time that you have to handle a situation that is significant in terms of how effectively you do your job. Include both times when things went well and times when they were less satisfactorily handled.

* * * * * * * * * * * * * * * * * *

1. Give a short factual description of what happened. (Who was involved? What was said and/or done? How long did it all take? What was the outcome?) _____

   _____

   _____

2. Was the outcome satisfactory? Very satisfactory/partly satisfactory/ unsatisfactory (*circle one*).
3. Describe what it was that made the outcome more or less satisfactory._____

   _____

   _____

4. Describe briefly any training you have received which you feel has helped you to deal with this particular incident. What difference has the training made? _____

   _____

   _____

5. Please mention any lack of training (or inadequate training you have experienced) which you feel has made it more difficult for you to handle the situation. _____

   _____

   _____

Figure 3.7 *Example of critical incident diary format*

Analysis of Critical Incident Data

It is desirable to have a proportion of incident diaries analysed by a second person as a check on the categorization of behaviours and a precaution against subjective judgements. The process of analysis goes through several steps.

Step 1

The incidents described on diary forms are sorted into those which provide clear descriptions of behaviour (verbal and physical) and those which are vague, lacking concrete detail or amount to inferences about things which could not be observed.

Step 2

Details within incidents should be linked to the training objectives that are being validated. There should be consensus amongst the validators about what is firm evidence for which objective. It may also be appropriate to use a statistical test of inter-rater reliability (see Chapter 6).

Step 3

The grouped examples of critical behaviours are compared to the original objectives. Frequencies are counted. Similarities between behaviour specified in the objective and that described in the critical incident provide reasonable evidence of linkage. Provided that a pre/post assessment has been made, changes in the relative proportions of 'good' and 'bad' behaviours offer evidence that the training is working. There may be reductions in the total number of critical incidents occurring or a shift from negatively-described occurrences to more with satisfactory outcomes. There may also be a shift from negative statements ('things to avoid') to positives ('things to do right'). If the training has been successful, there should be evidence that trained persons have learned how to apply the critical incident technique in order to become more as effective problem-solvers.

The Validation Interview

Interview is a one-to-one technique that is especially useful when you need to explore the inner workings of the trainee's mind – for example, the ways in which they have taken training inputs and applied them to specific work situations, or the ways in which they have found one method of learning more helpful than another. It is a valuable technique for follow-up validation to assess transfer of learning to work. Interview should not be confused with group discussions or feedback sessions such as are sometimes held at the end of a training course.

Interview is a risky technique to use, not least because superficially it appears a simple and informal method. Unfortunately, many people believe that one kind of interview is much the same as any other; this is not so, and people who conduct, say, successful recruitment interviews are prone to fail if they apply the same style of interviewing to the evaluation interview.

Because interview relies on the ability of the interviewee to recall and to analyse their own thought processes, there is the further risk that memory may be unreliable and that responses may be unintentionally or deliberately distorted. It therefore becomes very important that interviews are carefully structured, with pre-tested questions; that responses are tested by seeking concrete supporting evidence for the interviewee's statements; and that data recording and subsequent analysis do not themselves introduce any further bias, by interviewers who only hear what they want to hear. Unfortunately, unskilled interviewers are usually not aware of the effects they are having on respondents.

Telephone interviewing shares some of the advantages of face-to-face interviewing and is usually less costly and time-consuming. Response rates are usually good. However, it is much harder to establish rapport with the interviewee. Non-verbal indicators of the interviewee's feelings cannot be seen. Because it is difficult to keep a telephone interview going for as long as a face-to-face one, the range of questions has to be restricted. Opportunities for follow- up probing are diminished.

The elements of the validation interview are:

- designing the interview schedule;
- designing the system for processing the data collected;
- training the interviewers.

Designing the Interview Schedule

Step 1

An interview schedule is the equivalent of a test paper or behaviour observation instrument. It is a list of questions that will be asked, using exactly the same words, with every interviewee. This does not rule out ad hoc questions that follow-up or clarify particular responses but it does ensure consistency.

Decide what kinds of information you require. The key question to ask yourself is 'What do I really need to find out?' This should relate back to the learning objectives and to the particular aspects of the learning process that you want to explore. What must be resisted is the temptation to ask 'nice to know' questions which are not directly relevant to the task in hand. It can happen that, because access to some people in the organization is difficult, the validation interview is seen as an opportunity to ask supplementary questions that have nothing to do with the training in question. In the extreme, I have encountered situations (where interviewing had been delegated to field staff) where the original purpose of the validation interview has been almost wholly subverted by their pursuit of issues of local interest.

Plan to use as few questions as possible. Interview is an open-ended technique and answers tend to run on; 20 to 40 minutes is a good duration to aim for, both as a demand on the interviewee's time and in terms of the interviewer's span of attention. Aim for six to eight questions maximum in an interview schedule. Too many questions turn the interview into a verbal questionnaire and the depth of response required will be lost.

Watch out for questions that seek the same information using different words. At the drafting stage you should always ask yourself what would be likely answers to your question; you must then test this further at the trial-run stage.

A very important rule for question design is that your questions should be ones that your targeted respondents are likely to be able to answer. The questions must be on matters within their knowledge and experience. They need to understand the vocabulary that you employ. Bear in mind, too, that individuals differ in their ability to think introspectively, to generalize from experience, or to think in abstract terms.

Step 2

Determine the sequence of your interview schedule. Always begin by explaining the broad purpose of the interview and always be scrupulously careful not to give any hint of what you anticipate the conclusions might be. Respondents are usually very good at picking up cues and then telling you what they think you want to hear. Another opening element is to make clear the degree of confidentiality which will apply to the interview; a third is to explain how answers will be recorded (typically either by writing or tape-recording) for subsequent analysis.

The substantive questions should be grouped according to common themes and sequenced so that you move from more general initial questions to more focused follow-ups. Always ask questions about facts before you ask questions about feelings towards those facts. It is wise to move from the general and the innocuous to the specific and the controversial; first, because you should have built up more rapport with the interviewee by the later stages, and second because, if a difficult question leads to break- down of the interview, you will at least have covered the majority of topics by then.

Step 3

Use the correct types of question. In the free- flow of an interview it is easy to slip into using leading or rhetorical questions. *Leading* questions are worded so as to steer the respondent in the direction of a particular kind of answer, eg, 'Do you not feel that the management training could have been made more interesting if…'. *Rhetorical* questions have the format of a question, but are really statements which do not expect an answer.

Closed questions are those drafted in such a way that the answer will be short, specific and factual rather than explanatory in content, eg, 'What is your job title?' Such questions do not invite the respondent to expand their answer or to give conditional answers. There is only a limited use for the closed question within interview, to establish essential facts; if there are more than one or two closed questions, the interview opportunity is being wasted. You might just as well send a questionnaire by post.

When drafting closed questions, beware of creating false dichotomies of the type 'Do you do A or B?' when there are valid alternatives such as C or even D.

Open questions are intended to get the interviewee talking freely, but relevantly, eg, 'Can you please describe some examples of things that you now do differently because of the training?'. There is no single 'right answer' to open questions and answers will rarely be brief. There is the risk with open questions that interviewees may ramble inconsequentially, or that they may evade the question through verbiage. The former needs to be controlled by politely steering the dialogue back to matters in hand and moving to the next question.

Evasiveness arises for several reasons: not wanting to hurt the interviewer's feelings; not wanting to reveal that the interviewee has not used what was learned; or failure (during and after the training) to grasp what it was about. Evasiveness is usually evidenced by 'motherhood statements' – bland generalities of a vaguely positive nature, eg, 'That was a really good course. It changed my whole attitude to the job'. Responses like that invite a follow-up question of 'So what?' This key validation question is less bluntly and more fruitfully phrased in terms such as 'That's very interesting. Can you describe some actual instances where your change of attitude has made a difference to how you do your job?'. The value of interview as a validation technique hinges upon whether or not self-reported statements about the training 'working' can be underpinned by evidence of real changes in behaviour and identifiable results in the workplace.

Reflective questions are often very useful during validation interviews as a non-leading follow-up to an answer. They encourage the interviewee to say more – to clarify, or expand what has been said already. Reflective questions offer a more subtle way of probing into controversial areas than a direct question. They also provide a test of the accuracy of the interviewer's listening and enable the interviewee to correct any misunderstandings.

A reflective question consists of a short paraphrase or summary of what the interviewee has just said, delivered with a questioning intonation in your voice, eg, 'You said that there were different opinions about the purpose of that training course...'. It may be desirable to make the statement less threatening (and more of a check on what was said) by opening with a phrase such as 'I think you said...'.

Step 4

Draft the interview questions. Never take it for granted that what you have written is crystal-clear, unambiguous or to the point. Test every question on representatives of your target population. Listen to what they say: how they interpret the question, what answers they give (and how these compare to the answers you expected), how they feel about the interview as a whole.

Avoid words that will be interpreted differently by different interviewees, eg, frequently, most, never, all, adequately, positively. Watch out for words that may carry an emotional undertone that will bias the replies, eg, practical, academic.

Negative questions are confusing, eg, 'Do you not feel that the management training could have been made more interesting if...'. Double negatives are even worse, eg, 'Do you not feel that the management training could have been less uninteresting if...'.

Double-barrelled questions are also to be avoided. These are questions to which the interviewee may wish to answer 'yes' in one part and 'no' in the other, or may choose to answer one part as a way of avoiding answering the other, eg, 'Did you make use of what you had learned on the course – and how did your boss react to that?'.

Ask questions that are worded as invitations to provide facts, not as opportunities to indulge in self-justification. The easiest way to do this is to ask questions that use what, where, when, how, who – and not to ask why questions.

Step 5

Plan the administrative aspects of the interview process. It is preferable to interview the subjects on their home ground. Appointments (and possibly travel) need to be scheduled. An introductory letter should be drafted, to be sent to those in the interview sample even before appointments have been set up. The letter should describe the purpose of the validation exercise and invite their participation (rather than assume it). There should be a brief mention of the confidentiality of the interview (this issue can be handled more fully face-to-face). A confirmatory letter should be sent out after appointments have been made; this should emphasize the desirability (wherever practicable) of conducting the interview in a private office rather than in open-plan spaces.

Subject: Interviewing Skills Course

Interviewer................. Interviewee...................

Date...............

Introduction: Greeting and ice-breaking.

Purpose of the interview.

Written or taped record.

1. Please think back to before you attended the course. What did you expect to get out of the course?
2. Looking back, what, if anything, did you actually get out of it?
3. Did you draw up any kind of plan – either on paper or just in your own mind – to put into practice things that you had learned on the course? (Probe for details.)
4. Do you now do anything differently in your work as a result of the course?
5. Is there anything that you would like to do differently but you feel unable to put it into practice? (If yes, probe for details and explanation).
6. During the course, did you find the role plays a useful way of learning?
7. Do you have any comments you'd like to make about the style and methods of the course tutors?
8. Is there anything else that you would like to say about the course?

Close: thank interviewee.

Figure 3.8 *The interview schedule*

Step 6

The interview schedule should be given a dry run both with people who are experts on the subject matter that is being validated and with people who are similar to the target population of interviewees. It is useful to conduct the interview as if it were a real validation exercise, but after each question and answer pause to ask the interviewee to comment on his or her understanding of the question and feelings about answering it.

Ask interviewees how they might have worded the question. Take particular note of any areas of confusion, ambiguity, embarrassment, irritation, resistance, evasion or boredom. Watch with particular care for the interviewer needing to explain what questions mean; or for any tendency to argue with the answers, to talk too much or to justify the questions. Review the sequencing of questions. Were there any difficulties in recording data?

Step 7
Training the interviewers – see Chapter 5.

Step 8
Defining the sample – see Chapter 6.

Step 9
You have a choice about how you will record the responses that each interviewee gives you. It is usually not advisable to over-burden the interview relationship with a third person to act as scribe; it makes the event too formal and potentially threatening. Nor is it advisable to rely on memory alone, with notes written up at a later time. Although this method is good for building rapport, only the main details are likely to be remembered; indeed, selectively-biased recall is particularly likely with this method.

Making written notes as the interview proceeds is the least time-consuming, but usually not a very accurate method. It also has the substantial drawback that it gets in the way of building a good rapport between interviewer and subject. Eye contact is lost and a clip-board or desk can easily become a barrier between the parties. Furthermore, the pace of responses is likely to be slowed down by the writing speed of the interviewer (unless he or she possesses fluent shorthand). There is also the problem that answers to one question often contain useful information that 'belongs' under another heading; pressure to keep up with the flow of conversation may result in important information being ignored for reasons of convenience.

I recommend that tape recording of evaluation interviews is used wherever possible. Tape recording is often thought to be a controversial or high risk technique which may alienate interviewees. My experience is that objections are far more likely to come from inexperienced interviewers than from their subjects. Taping is usually acceptable provided it is introduced in the right way. What is unacceptable is secret taping of interviews.

Confidentiality must be discussed explicitly at the start of the interview and before taping starts. It is often easier to give credible guarantees when the evaluator is recognized to be an independent outsider rather than a member of, say, the corporate personnel department. You must say clearly who will have access to the recorded tape (preferably this should be solely the interviewer) and what will happen to the tape itself when the evaluation has been completed. Good practice is to ensure that tapes are electronically wiped once the data have been analysed; tapes must never be made available to managers or other third parties if promises have been made to protect the identity of respondents.

Tape-recording offers several advantages:

- it is much easier to maintain eye contact and build rapport with the interviewee;
- analysis of the taped data can be done under less pressure and the tape can be re-run as often as necessary to ensure accuracy. Nuances of tone and emphasis can be captured;
- the interviewer has much greater freedom to follow up answers with supplementary questions; instead of being tied up writing notes, the interviewer can actively participate in a two-way dialogue.

The main drawback of taping is its cost, especially the cost in terms of the time you need to make even a selective summary. A useful rule of thumb when transcribing tapes is to allow two to three times as long as the time occupied by the interview itself.

Step 10

The conduct of the interview is important not only for the success of that particular interaction but also for the reputation that will thereafter attach to the evaluation process as it rolls through the organization.

Start by greeting the interviewee by name, introduce yourself and smile. It can help to dress in a way that matches the style of interviewees. Break the ice with a few routine conversational pleasantries and then remind the interviewee of the purpose of the meeting, emphasizing how it will help improve training in the organization. Discuss the duration of the interview and try to ensure that it can be conducted without interruptions.

Talk about whether or not individual answers will be merged into group data; whether or not reported answers will be linked to named individuals; and what you can do to ensure that identity is not revealed by circumstantial information contained within an answer. If you use a word like 'confidential' then you should explain what you mean by it, in particular who, apart from yourself, may be involved in processing the interview data.

Progress through the interview schedule in the set order, using supplementary questions and probes to expand or clarify points of interest. Quite often, a question that you have not yet reached will be answered in the course of answering a previous question. It is generally advisable to ask the later question anyway, but to preface it with a remark such as 'I think you have touched on this point already, but I'd like to ask the question to be sure'.

The core skills of the interview are listening and maintaining rapport – a good relationship – with the interviewee. The relationship will quickly cool if you start to argue with the interviewee or pass judgements on what he or she has said. If you encounter clear discrepancies between what is said at different times within the same interview, try tactfully to clarify the interviewee's intentions rather than pounce on it as evidence of deliberate lying! Rapport is also lost if your attention appears to wander and you are perceived to be bored or annoyed. Rapport is strengthened by maintaining eye contact and by non-committal noises of encouragement whilst the interviewee is talking.

Occasional reflective summaries which demonstrate that you have listened accurately are a powerful aid to building the relationship. Careful listening – noting the tone as well as the words, the hints and undercurrents, even the things that are not said – is essential if the more subtle kinds of interview data are to be gathered. Valuable insights may be quite tentatively stated as a passing allusion or a 'throw-away remark' which can be easily missed.

Listening goes hand-in-hand with using the power of silence. When you have asked a question, wait. Silences always seem more uncomfortable for the questioner than for the interviewee. Also, silence gives the interviewee time to think about the answer and creates a pressure on them to give an answer. Try not to repeat your question just to fill the silence; above all, don't start to answer it yourself. During silences try to look attentive, maintain eye contact and create the impression that you are eager to hear the reply.

Another key use of silence is that you do not interrupt the flow of the interviewee's replies. Most interruptions are irritating and often interfere with the line of thought. However, interruptions are sometimes necessary where the interviewee has misunderstood the question or is rambling way off the topic.

End the interview with a general 'catch-all' question, eg, 'Is there anything else that you would like to say about…?' It very rarely adds any significant new information but it ensures that interviewees do not go away feeling that they have been prevented from saying what they wanted to say.

Conclude by thanking them for their cooperation and for the care they have taken to answer your questions. If necessary, offer reassurance about the confidentiality of their replies. Do not be tempted at this point into a discussion of your findings to date, or into comparisons triggered by a question from the interviewee such as 'How have you found my answers compared to other people's?'.

Step 11

Analysing the data from interviews can appear a more daunting task than the analysis of, say, test questions where the acceptable answers are clearly specified. However, valuable validation information can be discovered and the process is not unduly complicated. Three types of validation data are most likely to emerge from interviews: illustrative insights; frequency

Q4. Do you now do anything differently in your work as a result of the course? (Follow-up: How big a difference has that made?)				
CATEGORIES	RATING OF DIFFERENCE			
	Slight	Moderate	Large	No response
1. Plan daily work schedules more systematically	///	/////	//// ///// /////	/
2. Deal personally with customer complaints	///	/// /////	///// // ///	//
3.Etc.				
Totals	6	13	24	3

Figure 3.9 *An example of a frequency statements matrix*

Note: the example assumes that there were 23 interviewees.

statements; and statements of inferred causality and co-variance.

Illustrative insights can be very helpful to training designers and typically consist of an individual descriptive anecdote or a short case description, making a connection between some element of the training being validated and that individual's experience of the learning process or their subsequent work behaviour. The value of illustrative insights lies in their productive potential as ideas, not in being in any sense 'representative' or 'average' views. This type of insight is characteristic of the use of interview and open-ended questioning. Such data require little analysis. It may be important that identifying details are suppressed in order to protect anonymity. Statements of opinion or feeling should be supported by as much concrete detail of the circumstances as possible.

Frequency statements are arrived at by classifying and then counting the responses to interview questions, using a data matrix. Answers are grouped into categories which must be mutually exclusive, ie, there must be no overlap or ambiguity at the border between one category and another. The range of categories for each answer must also be comprehensive – it must allow for all possible responses that interviewees might make.

A simple example, using a closed question, might yield only two categories for analysis such as 'yes' and 'no'. A question about age groups might yield six categories (more or less are also possible), eg, under 21/ 21–30/31–40/41–50/51–60/61 and over

Note that overlap of categories would occur if the boundaries were drawn as 20 and under/20–30/30–40/40–50/50–60/60 and over.

Responses to a more complex open question may need to be analysed into several categories, each of which is itself sub-divided by a rating or grading (see Figure 3.9). Remember to include a 'no response' column.

To develop categories for analysing responses from interviewees, begin by reviewing the raw data – the notes or tape recordings compiled during interviews. Look for key words or short phrases that constitute an accurate summary of the point that the interviewee was making. If you cannot find good examples from the interviewee's own words, provide your own summarizing words or phrases; in this case, take great care that you really are summarizing what was said, not what you feel ought to have been said. These key words should represent the various ways in which interviewees have answered the question. As you progress through the data, start to bring key words together into logical groups which will become the analytical categories within a data matrix.

Simple frequency counts may be all you need to show that a training objective has (or has not) been achieved. Sometimes, however, you may also want to have some idea of what is 'typical' of the people surveyed. To do this, the categorized data can be further analysed to give a) the average and b) a measure of the central clustering. Depending on the type of data, the 'average' may be given by calculating the arithmetic mean, the median or the mode. The spread of responses is given by calculating range, quartile deviation or standard deviation. Methods of calculation are given in Chapter 6. You may wish to compare the data you have analysed for one group against that for another group (or for the same group on a different occasion). The appropriate technique is the chi-squared test, also described in Chapter 6.

Co-variation and causality: statistical correlation occurs where two or more groups of data vary together and this is measured by the Pearson coefficient of correlation (see Chapter 6 for details). Note that although a correlation between two variables means that you can predict that changes in one will be accompanied by changes in the other, such co-variance does not prove that one change *causes* the other.

To demonstrate a causal connection (to simplify the example, between X and Y), you need to show first that X and Y are correlated, ie, when one changes, the other changes also. These changes can be predicted from your working hypothesis about the causal link between X and Y. Second, you must show that the cause (say, X) occurs before the effect (say, Y). Third, you need to be able to 'draw a fence' around the correlation, so that no other factors can be responsible for the changes (eg, a third element Z, is the cause of the changes in both X and Y).

Validating Attitude Change by Repertory Grid

In Chapter 5 the argument is put for avoiding 'attitudes' altogether as a subject of training. For the benefit of anyone who finds it necessary to work within a framework of 'attitudinal' training objectives, the technique of repertory grid provides a basis for validation, with the advantage that it also encourages the conversion of attitudes to observable behaviours by trainees and trainers. The two usual training (as distinct from psycho-therapeutic) applications of repertory grid are as a pre-training diagnostic input to objective-setting and as a pre/post measure of changes brought about by some intervening training.

Repertory grid is derived from the personal construct theory of George Kelly, which states that each person has a unique framework for understanding the world, made up of personal constructs. Each construct is akin to an attitude (defined as a predisposition to act in a particular way) and provides a way of categorizing people and experiences.

Applied to validation of training, the use of repertory grid before and after training should show changes in the personal constructs used by trained persons. Of course, shifts in attitude do not automatically translate into shifts in behaviour, and therein lies the weakness of any attitude-based approach. However, repertory grid does allow users to define changes in their personal constructs in behavioural terms, provided they understand the attitude/behaviour distinction and choose to work with concrete and testable data rather than abstract and possibly wishful data.

The essence of the technique, in validation applications, is that trainees identify their personal constructs of 'good' and 'bad' applied to the subject of their training; eg, what are the differences between a good and a bad manager, a good and a bad selection interview, a good and a bad written report and so on. A useful feature of the technique is that the constructs that trainees generate are (or should be) entirely their own ideas, unfiltered by the hints, cues, assumptions and biases that can creep into even well- designed question-based techniques. At most, they can fruitfully be steered away from making vacuous or tautological distinctions ('A good manager is someone whom everyone looks up to') and towards distinctions about what a good or a bad manager does, or what they perceive the features of a good or bad object (such as a report) to be.

A blank repertory grid form (a) is given in Figure 3.10. The process generally takes about an hour to an hour-and-a-half for a group of trainees to complete.

Subject: Distinguishing features of...........................							
Description of *one* behaviour typical of the pair, but not of the third.	Six examples of .... that I am acquainted with.						Description of *one* behaviour typical of the third, but not of the pair.
	A	B	C	D	E	F	
	*	*	*				
	*		*	*			
	*			*	*		
	*				*	*	
		*	*	*			
		*		*	*		
		*			*	*	
			*	*	*		
			*		*	*	
	*	*		*			
		*	*		*		
			*	*		*	
	*	*			*		
		*	*			*	
	*	*				*	
	*		*		*		
	*			*		*	
	*		*			*	
		*		*		*	
			*	*	*		
				*	*	*	

Overall Ranking

Figure 3.10 *Repertory grid analysis form (a)*

Using the Grid Technique

Step 1

Identify what you want to use as the criterion for validating the training. This may be a global aim like 'become a better salesperson'; it can, but need not, be tied to detailed learning objectives. The task will then be to identify the differences between more competent and less competent salespeople in terms of what they do in their work-life that makes them better or worse.

Step 2

You will require six slips of paper (or small index cards) and a repertory grid analysis form (see Figure 3.10) for each person in the trainee group. Each group member must now identify six people who fit the category under analysis (in this example, salespeople). There should be a spread of ability within the six – ideally two very good, two poor, and two felt to be average performers. The most important criterion for selecting the six is that the trainee knows each one of the six well enough to be able to describe what it is that makes each more or less competent as a salesperson.

The six must be chosen individually by each group member and nobody needs to reveal publicly who their six names are. Any person's six may well include some people within that group, and different individuals' lists may well have names in common. It is possible for the individual doing the grid to include himself or herself as one of the six. (Indeed, when used as a self-development or diagnostic tool, the grid might include the person constructing the grid twice – once as they see themselves now and once as they would like to become). Each person should write down the names (or – often advisable – a coded substitute for the names), one name to a card.

Six is the number used here simply because trainees often find difficulty in thinking of more than six people whom they know well enough for the purpose of making comparisons. Eight or even ten people can be used, but the analysis becomes very protracted, and diminishing returns can be expected.

Step 3

Each trainee must shuffle their six slips and then label them A to F. On the analysis form, each horizontal row has three asterisks which appear under various combinations of the columns A to F. Starting with the top row, pick out the three name cards that correspond to A, B and C. (In the second row, you will pick out the cards labelled A, C and D, and so on).

Step 4

Place the three selected cards side by side and reflect upon the way the people they represent go about their work as salespeople. Try to identify what two of them have in common which also makes them different from the third. Look for a single, observable behaviour that characterizes these differences. Put the emphasis on the things that they would typically be seen or heard to do, not upon their personality traits or on inferences about their mental attitudes.

Write a brief phrase to describe the pair's common feature in the left-hand column; write the feature that differentiates the third salesperson in the right-hand column. Do not write anything in columns A to F. Take care that only one aspect of what the pair or the single person does is described. For example, 'researches clients and prepares visual aids' is a description of two separate behaviours. Note that the third person's differentiating behaviour may be the simple opposite or negative of what the other two do or it may be a related but different kind of response (see Figure 3.11)

When you are satisfied with the constructs that you have written in, return the cards to the pool.

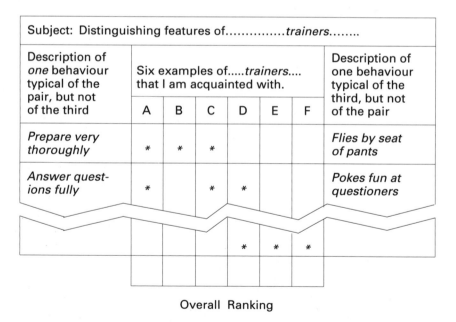

Overall Ranking

Figure 3.11 *Repertory grid analysis form (b)*

Step 5

Repeat the procedure at Step 4 for each of the rows in turn, or until you run out of differentiating constructs. You will need to be very familiar with your six subjects to be able to complete all 20 rows without repetition of constructs.

Step 6

Each row is now treated as a scale on which all six of your chosen examples can be ranked. Lay your six cards out in front of you. Start at the top row. Ask yourself:'Which of the six is most like the left-hand description?' Put a '1' in the column under the initial you have selected. Note that the one selected as most like the left-hand description need not be one of the original three who were used to develop that particular construct.

Next, decide which of the six is most like the right-hand description. Put a '6' in the column under that initial. Note that in a task like this one, it is easier to identify the most different examples first and the least distinguishable ones last. All six must be ranked 1 to 6; you cannot have tied positions.

Subject: Distinguishing features of...............*trainers*........							
Description of *one* behaviour typical of the pair, but not of the third.	Six examples of.....*trainers....* that I am acquainted with.						Description of one behaviour typical of the third, but not of the pair.
	A	B	C	D	E	F	
Prepare very thoroughly	2 *	3 *	6 *	5	1	4	*Flies by seat of pants*
Answer quest- ions fully	4 *	3	1 *	5 *	6	2	*Pokes fun at questioners*
				*	*	*	

Overall Ranking

Figure 3.12 *Repertory grid analysis form (c)*

Now select the example that is second most like the left- hand construct and put a '2' in the appropriate column. Likewise, a '5' for the second most like to the right-hand construct. Finally, allocate the '3' and '4' positions in the same way. The analysis form should now look something like the example in Figure 3.12.

Carry on with the ranking process, one row at a time, until each row has been dealt with. Shuffle the name cards after each row so that you do not inadvertently impose an order that simply reflects the way they are laid out.

Step 7

Rank all six examples in terms of your judgement of their overall effectiveness (however you yourself happen to think of that). Use '1' for most effective and '6' for least effective and so on. Enter this 1 to 6 ranking in the row of boxes at the very bottom of the analysis form, which should now look something like the example in Figure 3.13.

Subject: Distinguishing features of...............*trainers*........							
Description of *one* behaviour typical of the pair, but not of the third.	Six examples of.....*trainers*.... that I am acquainted with.						Description of one behaviour typical of the third, but not of the pair.
	A	B	C	D	E	F	
Prepare very thoroughly	2 *	3 *	6 *	5	1	4	*Flies by seat of pants*
Finishes on time	1	3	4	5	2	6	*Cuts sessions*
	3	2	5	6	1	4	

Overall Ranking

Figure 3.13 *Repertory grid analysis form (d)*

Step 8

The last stage is to correlate your rankings on each personal construct with your overall ranking of effectiveness for the six examples. Take a piece of scrap paper and copy the 'overall effectiveness' rankings onto it, carefully aligning the copy with the A to F columns. Then, overlay the copy against the ranking in the first row of the analysis form. Within each of the columns A to F, subtract the smaller number from the larger (see Figure 3.14).

| Prepare very thoroughly | 2 * | 3 * | 6 * | 5 | 1 | 4 | Flies by seat of pants |

SCRAP PAPER OVERLAY

| | | 3 | 2 | 5 | 6 | 5 | 4 | |

Calculation of differences:

Column	Larger Value	Smaller Value	Difference
A	3	2	1
B	3	2	1
C	6	5	1
D	6	5	1
E	1	1	0
F	4	4	0
Sum of differences			4

The sum of differences is added across each row. Write the sum in a circle on the margin of the analysis sheet. Carry on, moving the overlay paper down row by row.

Figure 3.14 *Repertory grid analysis form (e)*

Step 9

Inspect the circled difference-totals for any high scores (12 and above). High scores indicate one of two possibilities. One is that the personal constructs on that row do not correlate with overall effectiveness: you may see those constructs as a means of differentiating the three examples within that row, but you do not see those constructs as contributing to the effectiveness of the examples. For example, trainers D and E might be linked by wearing smart suits, whereas trainer B apparently dresses from a charity shop; however, you do not see their style of clothing making any difference to the learning of the particular groups of trainees that B, D, and E work with, because all of them use distance learning methods rather than face-to-face tuition.

The second possibility flagged by a high sum of differences is that on that row the pair is linked by a construct that describes negative behaviour or features and the single example is identified by a positive construct.

The task now is to reverse the row scores, so that 6 becomes 1, 5 becomes 2, and 4 becomes 3. Then re-calculate the sum of differences between the row scores and the overlay. This may bring the high score down to a low level which indicates a close correlation between the constructs and your judgement of overall effectiveness.

Step 10

Discard all constructs where the sum of differences for that row is 4 or more. Low scores (0–3) indicate that the constructs correlate closely with your judgement of overall effectiveness.

Note, incidentally, that the whole repertory grid technique works with *perceptions* of effectiveness; if your ideas of what makes for an effective manager – or whatever – are eccentric or confused, the grid analysis will reflect this. It does, though, bring into the open your perceptions and misconceptions, in a way that enables you to work on them subsequently; hence the value of the technique as a diagnostic tool in self-development applications.

To use the data for validation purposes, you will need to run the repertory grid process with the trainees before and after the training. As with any pre/post assessment, the trainees should not have access to the results of the pre-test before they have taken the post-test. Comparisons can be made in terms both of changes in group and individual results. With a group, firstly compile a combined list made up of the two lowest scoring constructs from each member. For an individual comparison, use all of that person's low- scoring constructs.

The expectation, if training has been successful, is that trainees will have a clearer understanding of the subject and of the ways in which it contributes to their doing an effective job. In the pre/post comparison, you would therefore expect to see a number of changes:

- there should be more constructs with a low sum-of-differences score (more 0s and 1s; fewer 3s and 4s);
- the constructs used should be more precise, concrete rather than abstract, focused upon observable behaviour rather than inferred personality traits;
- there should be much more consensus within a group about what is meant by 'being an effective trainer (or report, or whatever)'.

4 **Practical Tests**

▷   SUMMARY   ◁

- Practical tests need to be used wherever a trainee is required to put new knowledge to use in either a technical or a clerical/administrative application. Such tests may be used to measure the output of a task (the finished product) or the process by which it was accomplished.
- Tests must reflect the different types of skill that training imparts. Skills can be classified by level of complexity and any particular test may set out to measure one or several of these four levels:

  – simple recall and identification;
  – procedure-following;
  – problem-solving and analytical tasks;
  – manual dexterity.

- The use of in-tray exercises as a validation method is discussed because these offer a powerful technique for assessing how well managerial, supervisory, sales or administrative skills can be put to use in a realistic simulation.
- The steps in designing the practical test are described in full detail, including the choice of 'closed book' or 'open book' testing and the setting of standards of acceptable performance. The distinction between norm-referenced and criterion-referenced measures is clarified.

Introduction

It is rare to find practical tests in use outside the training centre, partly because specialized equipment may be involved, partly because tests provide a simulation whereas the workplace provides the 'real thing' and the latter may be too dangerous or otherwise impracticable for testing purposes. Practical tests can be used for pre/post validation of training, as an initial diagnostic aid and as a terminal measure of competence for certification purposes. As a diagnostic aid, tests can identify those parts of the subject area in which the trainee is already competent or can establish what the pre-requisite levels of knowledge or skill may be for entry to the training.

Practical tests need to be used wherever a trainee is required to put new knowledge to use in either a technical or a clerical/administrative application. The use of behaviour observation (see Chapter 3, pp. 44) is of course a form of practical test, but it is sufficiently different in nature to justify separate treatment.

Written tests and practical tests may be used in a complementary fashion as the trainee's knowledge and skills develop stage-by-stage. However, written tests can never be a wholly adequate substitute for a practical test which demonstrates whether or not a trainee can carry out some skilled task.

Practical tests may be used to measure the output of a task or the process by which it was accomplished. Output may be assessed in terms of quality standards (whether turning metal on a lathe, or preparing a report on a word-processor); process in terms of planning ability, speed of working, safety practices, anticipation of problems, etc.

Practical tests are usually well-received by trainees because they are perceived to be relevant (that is, they have high face-validity), and provide rapid feedback on how well the individual is progressing. Other advantages are that they reinforce learning by providing additional skill practice and, by giving a realistic simulation, they help bridge the transfer of learning to the workplace. On the downside, practical tests can be time-consuming and may be expensive to create, especially where equipment is involved, and particularly where that equipment may be put at risk of damage. Realistic simulation may be difficult, or simply very costly. Tests often need to be closely supervised, using direct observation. At the same time, it may be difficult to prevent trainees observing each other during the test period.

Classifying Skills for Testing

Skills can be classified into different levels of complexity and any particular test may set out to measure one or several of these levels. A useful way of classifying skills is that provided by P. Harmon (*Educational Technology*, January 1969) (Figure 4.1).

---

1. VERBAL
    Level 1.1: recall; listing; stating fact or rule.
    Level 1.2: explaining procedure.
    Level 1.3: responding to questions or statements.
    Level 1.4: solving a specific problem.
    Level 1.5: solving a general class of problem.
2. PHYSICAL
    Level 2.1: identifying physical objects.
    Level 2.2: performing simple physical actions.
    Level 2.3: performing more complex physical actions either whilst following instructions or from memory.
    Level 2.4: performing physically-skilled actions.
    Level 2.5: selecting an appropriate action and performing it.
    Level 2.6: determining acceptable quality in physical products.

Figure 4.1: *Classification of performance objectives*

A test may consist of several items all of which measure attainment on one particular level of skill; alternatively, the test may be a complex activity in which the trainee has to demonstrate competence at several levels, partly occurring in a logical sequence, partly occurring simultaneously. For example, a person operating, say, a biscuit-cutting machine, would need to be able to identify all control knobs (2.1), follow a start-up procedure (2.3), watch out for faulty products (2.6) and trouble-shoot when something goes wrong (2.5, probably with 2.2 or 2.3).

The test may focus on the final output – boxed biscuits, sales letter, etc., which requires less assessor time, or it may involve a step-by-step assessment of each stage, with the benefit that corrective feedback can be given.

The list of levels of performance objective in Figure 4.1 can effectively be condensed down to four categories. These are:

1. Simple recall and identification (levels 1.1; 1.3; 2.1)
2. Procedure-following (1.2; 2.3; 2.4)
3. Problem-solving and analytical tasks (1.4; 1.5; 2.5; 2.6)
4. Manual dexterity (2.2; 2.3; 2.4; 2.5)

Group 1

The first of these four groups requires the trainee to recall from memory, or to recognize when displayed, objects or words or graphic symbols. It includes the trainee giving simple factual answers to questions.

EXAMPLES

What is this part of the lathe called?

What is the function of the 'Num Lock' key?

What does this symbol represent?

An extended example of recall testing is given in the next example.

EXAMPLE

Recall/identification test (test item)

Instructions to the trainee: write on the blank lines the name of each of the parts indicated by arrows in the drawing below. You have five minutes to complete this. You will be assessed on accuracy and on spelling.

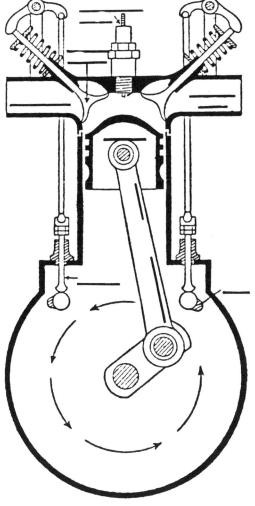

OVERHEAD VALVE ENGINE
ON COMPRESSION STROKE

Answers to test item

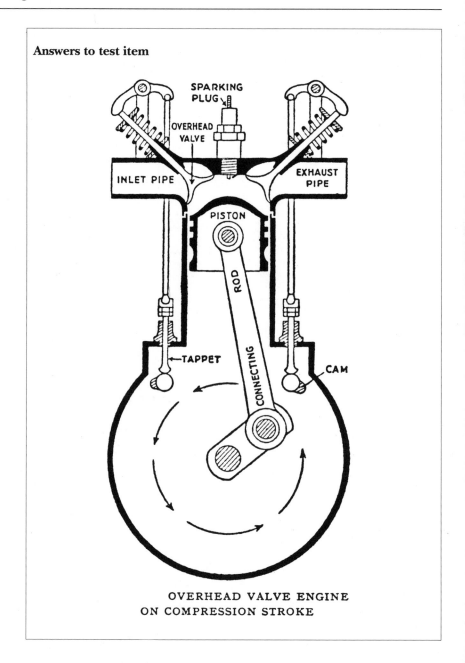

OVERHEAD VALVE ENGINE
ON COMPRESSION STROKE

Group 2

The second group tests the trainee's ability to explain a procedure or to follow a sequence of actions (either from memory or aided by prompting).

EXAMPLES

Describe the correct procedure for removing a car wheel.

Re-assemble this water pump.

What do you do with a new life insurance proposal form?

Print out, in date order, all purchase orders received from XYZ Ltd since 1 January 1992.

Make the entries to find out which flights have seats available from Amsterdam to London early on the morning of October 17th. Print out the result.

An extended example is given below.

EXAMPLE

Procedure items

Use the order terminal to obtain the information you need in order to complete all the items marked * on the customer order form shown below. You have 10 minutes to complete this.

XYZ (Wholesalers) Ltd
The Business Park
Ambridge
XYl 2XZ   ORDER FORM
Customer: *   Delivery Address: *

Order No. 927985		Customer No.*		
Date*		Customer Ref.*		
Item No.	Description	Unit	Quantity Ordered	Quantity Delivered
23AOB95	*	box	10	
*	Grn.Sq.Cut	100	*	
89ABF42	*	*	*	

Group 3

In the third group, the range of test items includes:

- use of an algorithm (decision-tree);
- diagnosis of deliberately-created faults in equipment;
- sorting and responding to material in an in-tray (in a sales, managerial or clerical context);
- making judgements about the quality of processes or outputs.

EXAMPLE

Using the information in the case study provided, apply the algorithm to decide the claim for compensation.

Locate and replace the faulty circuit board.

Given an in-tray comprising company reports, previous correspondence, internal memoranda and telephone messages, prepare an action plan for your next sales call.

Examine the carpentry test piece and state, with reasons, whether or not the quality is to specified standards.

Most test items of this kind are self-evident; their selection reflects expert knowledge of the subject area, shaped by local requirements and procedures. However, it is worth looking in more detail at the use of in-tray tests which, though quite common in recruitment and promotion exercises, are less often found in use for validation purposes, although they offer a strong technique for assessing whether or not management, supervisory, sales or administrative skills have been internalized and can be put to use in a realistic simulation.

The test will consist of a tray of items – typically letters, memos, phone messages, reports and the like – which have some close relationship to the objectives of the training. The subsequent validation exercise may be wholly paper-based, with trainees producing written responses to in-tray materials; but it is often preferable to incorporate elements of behavioural assessment as well. Written responses can be combined with observed role plays and group activities.

Scoring of in-tray validations follows the same rules as for tests and for behaviour observation. Both process and product assessments may be made. Scoring may be tied to productivity (how many items are dealt with), to prioritizing (whether the trainee handles the more important or urgent items first) and to the quality of responses. Scoring must be tied to specified actions and defined standards of performance. Otherwise, the method is very prone to degenerate into scoring by 'general impressions', where assessors make up their mind about who is good or bad and then back-fit the scoring to rationalize their intuitive judgements.

Group 4

The fourth group ranges from simple physical actions, such as driving a nail, to complex sequences of action which may combine Group 3 diagnostic skills with high levels of manual dexterity, eg, repairing a watch.

Test items will require the trainee to make, assemble, dismantle, manipulate, repair or process artifacts, tools, measuring and diagnostic instruments. Scoring may be weighted, if it is valid to categorize some parts of the task as more critical to success (or safety) than others.

Designing the Practical Test

Step 1

As always, try to develop test items in parallel with the development of learning objectives. In practical testing, a defined standard of performance and specified conditions for performance are both particularly important – it may be a very different experience carrying out a task in workshop conditions compared to carrying it out 'in the field'. By developing test items from task-based training objectives, you ensure a close correspondence with the jobs for which people are being trained and enhance transfer of learning.

Note, however, the quite common problem (mostly with technical training) that whereas instruction is given 'by the book', experienced workers often cut corners and, sometimes, a whole alternative 'local way of doing things' evolves. This does present a problem for the credibility of trainers and for the effectiveness of testing, although the solution to the problem lies with management rather than with training. The real issue concerns whether or not the organization will formally condone this pluralist approach – in which case training can respond with activities tailored to local variations in practice – or will grasp the supervisory and disciplinary nettle of enforcing a common approach throughout the organization. (This is a different kind of issue, shaped by technical and safety considerations, from the pluralism often found in sales departments, where different styles of selling may be employed with different kinds of customer).

Step 2

The actions to be performed in the test must be specified as precisely as possible. There should be no room for interpretation about what the test entails. Compliance with safety procedures should be included in the task specification and a proportion of marks should be awarded for good practice.

The test may set out to assess the final product or service – the output – or the process by which that output was achieved or some combination of both. With process items, the trainee must be observed throughout the test period (the assessment itself can, in principle, be deferred, if the process is recorded using video). With physical outputs, though not service outputs, the assessment may be carried out at a separate time and place.

When designing process items, there are some key rules to follow:

- each item must be observable, not, ever, an inference about what someone might be thinking;
- items should be worded so as to yield a yes/no, present/absent distinction, rather than a scaled response;
- each test item must focus on only one process element;
- subjective terms such as 'satisfactory', 'properly', 'well', should be avoided
- where certain items have particular importance (eg, safety precautions) it may be appropriate to instruct the trainee to pause at that point in order that the instructor can check whether or not the processes have been correctly completed

Product test items have their own design features, additional to those listed for process items:

- each must be capable of precise specification – whether this is a matter of engineering tolerances or the moisture content of a biscuit or the core elements of a sales proposal;
- each item must only be assessed on criteria that are critical to its effectiveness (eg, for routine correspondence the Fog Index is a relevant measure, whereas whether the paper is z-folded or u-folded is not; on the other hand, for sales letters, z-folding may be a relevant criterion to apply);
- product items may need to have 'pause' stages built into the test because there may be certain points in the test process beyond which physical inspection becomes impossible without destroying the workpiece (eg, when something is being assembled, or a sealed joint is being created).

Step 3

A marking scheme should be drawn up in parallel with defining the test tasks. This scheme will state which elements of performance will count for however many marks. Note that marks are awarded only for performance elements, not for personality.

The conditions and standards of performance should also be specified. There is no value in secrecy about the basis on which trainees will be assessed. 'Conditions' may include the location in which the test occurs; the availability of tools and materials; whether or not prompting by the tester is allowed (and the deductions that will be made from total marks, if prompting is required); the time available for completion; and whether or not the test will be run 'closed book' or 'open book'.

Location is significant for some kinds of task: repairing a leaking pipe in a workshop is likely to be a different kind of experience to the same task performed in a trench in the middle of a busy trunk road. The pressures, hazards and distractions will not be the same and the importance of these factors to effective job performance should be considered when planning the training and its associated tests.

In a closed-book test, the trainees have to carry all the information they need in their heads. In an open-book test, they are allowed access to specified reference material (eg, course notes; technical manuals; codes of practice; legal references; etc.). Which approach is appropriate depends upon the learning objectives and hence upon the nature of the task. Where information needs to be available in the course of carrying out activities, it may be essential to hold that information in memory. For example, a learner driver needs to memorize road signs. In other situations, it may be preferable, or essential, that workers check what they are doing against written procedures (corporate or statutory); in such instances, their ability to find their way around the reference sources is the key skill that needs to be tested, and the open book-method is needed.

Standards of acceptable performance need to be stated. The basic distinction is between norm-referenced and criterion-referenced measures. Norm-referenced standards compare each trainee against other members of the trained population; a cut-off 'fail' standard is set by reference to the proportion of the whole population that the assessors want to pass, eg, the bottom 40 per cent will be failed. This method is typified by the old '11-plus' examination but has little value in training where the intention is to get everyone up to an acceptable standard, rather than to competitively allocate scarce resources.

Criterion-referencing measures attainment against a pre-set standard that should closely reflect the nature of the task for which testing is occurring. The standard is generally a matter of judgement, although statute and codes of practice may sometimes shape it and the trend towards codes of 'customer service' will also set a number of standards. A standard of 80 per cent is often cited as an 'acceptable' pass level by trainers attending my workshops, but this is an arbitrary figure reflecting at best actual current levels of attainment, rather than targets.

It may be argued that 100 per cent is the only acceptable level. Certainly, the emphasis on 'right first time' as a quality standard in both manufacturing and service sectors supports that. Anything less than 100 per cent implies that the test item is not too critical and does open up the option of a hierarchy of test items of differing levels of importance. This has to be a judgement based upon knowledge of the tasks in question. Eighty per cent might be deemed acceptable when training labourers to plant trees; 98 per cent deemed unacceptable when training a pilot to land an aircraft. In general, test standards should be comparable to those expected from experienced workers, but trainees should be allowed more time in which to complete the task.

Step 4

Devise a standardized administration of the test so that all trainees experience the same introductory instructions about the test, the same level of supervision, the same physical environment and the same time constraints. Instructions to trainees may be written or given verbally, using a standard script to ensure consistency between tests. Instructions should specify:

- purpose of the test;
- conditions under which the test will occur;
- time limit for completion;
- what the trainee is required to do – emphasizing critical points and safety requirements;
- criteria for success.

The test environment only needs to be as realistic a simulation of working conditions as is necessary to ensure that the test is a valid assessment device. Environmental realism does become particularly important when training for emergency and high-risk activities; sometimes it may be necessary to accept less realism in the test as a necessary trade-off against unacceptable hazard levels.

Step 5

Conduct trial runs of the test and the marking scheme. Amend where necessary to eliminate any confusions in what the test entails and any ambiguities in the listed actions or outputs for which marks may be awarded. Where there may be several people involved in the marking, it is important that they cross-mark the same test results and that any discrepancies in scoring are investigated and resolved. By the time that the test is used with 'live' training groups, there should be no scope for discretionary marking. In those practical tests which involve observation of the test process, the guidelines on training assessors for behaviour observation techniques may be found helpful (see Chapter 5, pp. 88).

Step 6

Practical testing may be used simply as a pre/post measure of a group of learning objectives. However, it is also useful when used at each stage of learning, especially when a 'part-whole' structure is being employed. Ideally, proficiency should then only be tested when the trainee feels ready to move on to the next part. Note that where a learning task is very complex, or especially important, the trainee should be required to demonstrate competence several times, under different circumstances or in different applications, before proceeding further.

5 General Topics

┌───┐

▷   SUMMARY   ◁

- Several diverse topics relating to validation are gathered together in this chapter.
  The first section discusses the training needed for people who are conducting
  behaviour observation, the second training for testing, and the third focuses on
  those who carry out validation interviews. The fourth section presents designs for
  workshops to introduce a) managers and b) trainers to validation ideas and
  techniques. The fifth reviews the issue of attitudes versus behaviour in training
  design. The final section examines the limitations and uses of end-of-course
  reactions data - the ubiquitous 'happy sheet'.

└───┘

Training for Behaviour Observation

The Sole Trainer

This is not easily accomplished by the trainer working alone; effective
learning benefits greatly if there are two or more people working together
to observe real or role-played interactions. The differences in what each
person observes provides a very fruitful basis for discussion about accurate
observation and the problems of interpreting behaviour categories.

The trainer working in isolation can make the best of a difficult
learning situation by using a test/retest method, in which the individual
compares the results of a behaviour observation exercise at one point in
time with the results of the same exercise at a later date. Inconsistencies
in behaviour categorization may then be apparent and can be corrected.

Video material can be used to good effect as an observer training aid. Almost any piece of film, whether depicting work situations or fiction can be used to practise developing an observation instrument and then applying that to the material. Better still is to use video recordings of training sessions, particularly if material is available that relates to the types of behaviour for which the observer is being trained.

Training a Group of Observers

A group of observers can be trained, following the steps outlined below.

Step 1

Describe to the trainee observers what the skills are that the training which they will observe has been designed to develop. Describe these skills in behavioural terms and with as much specific detail as possible. Describe the behaviour categories that appear on the observation checklist that the trainee observers will be using. Spell out clearly the connection between each category on the checklist and the behavioural training objective to which it relates. Emphasize that observers have the task of recording occurrences and non-occurrences of behaviour rather than of making judgements about the quality of performance. (My view is that all you need to know is whether or not the right behaviours have been exhibited. If you add a rating score on top of that factual information, all you are really doing is making a judgement about whether or not you like that individual. Note the rating errors described in Step 2!).

Step 2

Practise the application of each category in turn to examples of behaviour. The trainees may start off doing this with simple written transcripts of verbal interactions, before moving on to more complex interactions and to 'live' observation of video or role play. At each stage of this process, the trainee observers' categorizations must be checked. The differences between trainee observers' interpretations and those of experienced observers provide a fruitful basis for discussion. Practice should continue until the trainees can work quickly and accurately and cope with increasing numbers of behaviours and/or more observed subjects at any one time.

Some common sources of error if observers use ratings of performance as well as (or instead of) factual observations of 'did the behaviour happen?' type, are the following:

- *Halo Effect:* the tendency of observers to generalize from one well-performed action to the whole of the person's behaviour.
- *Generosity Error:* where observers (mostly, unconsciously) give better results for trainees whom the observers feel are similar to

89

themselves; the opposite effect is produced by the *Contrast Error*, where the observer 'marks down' because of a perception that the trainee is opposite in character to the observer.
 – *Moderation Error:* the tendency to give central values on a rating scale and to avoid the extreme values of good and bad

Step 3
Trainee observers work in parallel with experienced observers during 'live' training events. The reliability of their work can be compared to that of the experienced observers and, if necessary, further training provided. Observers must become not only accurate in categorizing behaviours but also accurate in attributing any observed behaviour to the right person in the observed interaction.

Reliability in Behaviour Observation

Reliability in behaviour observation has three aspects:

 – inter-rater reliability, which is the consistency between one observer and another when both observe the same piece of behaviour;
 – test/retest reliability, which is the consistency achieved between one occasion of using an observation instrument and another;
 – sampling reliability, which concerns whether the range of behaviours within an observed interaction are adequately represented by the observation process.

Reliability is measured by comparing the rank-order correlation of two sets of observations (using Spearman's rho, see Chapter 6). The extent of difference between two observers is given by the correlation coefficient.

Training of Testers

Written tests require relatively little pre-training of the testers. All the potential difficulties should have been sorted out in the design of the test itself and the complementary marking scheme. The main training requirement is then to ensure standardized administration of the test, including appropriate control of reference materials in the case of open-book tests.

For practical tests, guidance may be needed on safety matters and on the extent of prompting that is allowed during the test. Otherwise, where practical tests involve the observation of trainees behaviour as they carry out tasks, all the issues discussed above, under training for behaviour observation, will apply.

A secondary tester-training requirement concerns the way in which tests and test results are presented to trainees – memories of school may be an obstacle for some people facing tests in adult life. Intra-group rankings may sometimes be a problem, especially if there is a well-entrenched culture of equal status within the group. The use of gain ratios rather than raw scores (see Chapter 6) can help here, as will the avoidance of any public ranking of the people tested. The way in which feedback is provided will make the difference between positive reinforcement of learning and rejection of the message because of the messenger's delivery.

Practice in use of tests can be obtained by analysing the data from tests conducted by more experienced trainers; by shadowing experienced testers; and by acting as guinea pigs when new tests are piloted.

Rules for Giving Feedback

The rules for giving trainees feedback apply to all forms of validation testing. These rules are:

- Feedback should help the learner, not serve as an excuse for the trainer to let off steam; reinforcement of good practices through praise is even more important than correction of errors.
- Feedback should be given as soon as possible after the observed behaviour has occurred.
- If trainees are to make use of feedback, they must understand it, so keep comments specific, rooted in concrete detail and in plain English.
- Do not confuse facts with opinions, and do not present your judgements as if they were facts.
- Focus comments upon the observed actions of the trainee, not upon personality characteristics (real or inferred) and invite suggestions from the trainee about how improvements might be made.
- Only make comments about performance on the basis of criteria that have previously been set for the activity.

Training for Validation Interviewing

The three core elements of successful validation interviewing are:

- ask the questions that appear on the interview schedule;
- remain silent; and
- listen to (and accurately record) the answers.

USE OF QUESTIONS	FREQUENCY OF USE	SPECIFIC EXAMPLES
Open		
Closed		
Reflective		
Leading		
USE OF INTERVIEWING BEHAVIOURS	FREQUENCY OF USE	SPECIFIC EXAMPLES
Inaccurate listening		
Reflective summarising		
Use of silence		
Interruption		
Clarification		

Figure 5.1: *Observer's checklist for validation interview practice*

The interview schedule will consist of questions that relate to the learning objectives of the training that is being validated. These questions should have been thoroughly tested and revised during pilot interviews. It is not, then, a good idea to re-word the questions for each interview, to omit questions or to change the order of questions. The purpose of validation is subverted and you lose consistency between your interviewees.

This is not to say that ad hoc follow-up questions are not to be used: these can clarify the subject's statements or explore new lines of thought that have emerged in the course of the interview. But follow-up questions are always supplementary to the interview schedule, not a substitute for the pre-planned questions.

Silence is a powerful and necessary tool for the interviewer. When you have asked a question, zip it! Remain attentive, with eye contact and try to convey non-verbally that you are keen to hear the reply. Be comfortable about waiting for an answer. The silence always seems longer and more anxiety-provoking to the questioner than to the interviewee (who is probably using the space to sort out an answer). Never start to answer the question yourself! Only restate the question if the interviewee asks you to.

It is also important to maintain silence when the interviewee is talking; make vague, encouraging noises that show you are listening, but do not interrupt the flow (unless the conversation has gone wildly off-track).

Listening is the most important skill of all. At least 95 per cent of the talk should be coming from the interviewee; interviewers should never, ever get drawn into a debate about the subjects under validation. People are very adept at shaping their answers to fit whatever they perceive you want to hear, so avoid giving clues – either accurate or misleading ones.

Accurate listening is not a passive process; it requires interviewers to check out regularly the accuracy of what they think they have heard, using reflective summaries. Accurate listening also requires that the interviewer hears the bad news as well as the good. It is the interviewee's point of view that matters and that should not be filtered and sanitized by the interviewer's preferences or prejudices.

Interviewing skills can be usefully practised in groups of three, with one person acting as observer of the interview. An observation checklist is provided (see Figure 5.1) for your use in such role plays. This exercise also offers an opportunity to experience giving and receiving feedback.

Validation Workshops for Managers and Trainers

When proper validation of training is introduced, it is a form of culture change, just as much as programmes to change management style or to introduce 'quality'. As always, that means there is a lot of inertia and sometimes opposition to overcome. Making changes happen is partly a matter of knowing where you want to go and partly a matter of exercising political skills that build your support (and resourcing).

Validation efforts create a momentum of their own. They build up the credibility of the training function. They show that trainers are seriously trying to create effective training, rather than pretending that nothing requires improvement.

Validation is more likely to take root if the majority of people in a particular training unit or training department are working within a common frame of reference. However, people take time to absorb new ideas and this has two implications. One is for the timescale over which validation is introduced; the other (for training managers) is that they must act positively to build a momentum of changed practice. Ownership of validation projects by trainers and managers is vitally important.

SKILLS DEVELOPMENT	ORGANIZATIONAL CONTEXT
Initial workshop to open up debate and establish pilot projects.	Gaining commitment from policy-makers. Creating a dialogue with line managers.
Acquisition of validation skills, primarily by trainers.	Reviewing training strategy. Establishing administrative procedures.
Routine use of validation, plus updating of skills.	Leadership: – active goal-setting; – rewarding validation activities: – acting on validation findings.

Figure 5.2: *Introducing validation into an organization*

There are two parallel changes (Figure 5.2) that need to occur during the period when validation is being introduced. Trainers must themselves become skilled in use of the techniques. At the same time, policy changes are often needed to create a climate in which validation is seen as useful and is encouraged.

As well as bringing the training department up to speed, it is essential that management at all levels becomes involved. Senior managers quite often make remarks that are intended to support training. They then go on to undermine their words through behaviour that contradicts the message. The commitment of senior policy-makers to a training strategy is valuable, but it is many times more useful if it translates into influence and rewards that encourage middle and junior managers to play an active role in the training partnership: people in organizations do the things which they are rewarded for doing.

In many organizations, the first step will be to unfreeze set attitudes – particularly defensive fear of validation – and to counter the common perception that validation is a good idea in theory but too difficult in practice. What follows are the outline designs for three workshops typical of events that I have run successfully for a wide range of organizations over the years. The workshops can, of course, be adapted to your local needs.

Workshop 1: a short introduction to strategy, evaluation and validation ideas.

Workshop 2: covering both techniques and project implementation (five days over about three months).

Workshop 3: a short workshop for managers on ways that they can contribute to making training more effective.

WORKSHOP 1

A Short Introduction to Strategy, Evaluation and Validation Ideas

Learning objectives

At the end of the workshop, participants will be able to:

- Describe key issues in training strategy, validation and evaluation.
- Describe and use a framework for determining what they want to assess.
- Select techniques for specific applications.
- Prepare a first draft of at least one type of instrument, to a standard that is likely to require additional work before it is suitable for implementation.

Topics

Introduction:

- Why do strategy and evaluation go hand-in-hand?
- What is training strategy about?
- Manager-trainer collaboration.
- Systematic training design.
- Quality assurance in training.
- Catalysing change.
- Evaluation and validation.

Outline of main techniques of validation and evaluation

- Reactionnaire
- Interview
- Questionnaire
    Exercise: drafting an interview schedule for a specific application.
- Cost-benefit analysis
    Exercise: bottom-line penalties of competence gaps.
- Testi..g, written and practical.
- Repertory grid.

– Behaviour observation.

Exercise: drafting a short behaviour observation checklist to assess the use of a specified aspect of interpersonal skills in the workplace.

Putting the project together.

WORKSHOP 2
Techniques and Project Implementation

Purpose

To introduce personnel and training practitioners to practical methods by which they can assess the effectiveness of training within their organisation. The workshop is designed for:

– Personnel and training managers.
– Experienced and newly-appointed trainers.
– Line managers with training responsibilities.

Participants should have some direct involvement in training design or delivery to provide the basis – during the term of the workshop – for an individual or team-based project.

The workshop is designed for groups of up to 12 people and it is recommended that the training manager should always participate.

Structure of the evaluation programme

– An initial two days of tutor input and practical design work.
– A half-day follow-up 7-10 days later.
– A one-day follow-up about 8–10 weeks later (timing determined by the timetable of training activities within the company).
– Telephone support to participants during the project stages.

Content of the programme

–Initial workshop.

Training strategy and effectiveness.
Purposes and benefits of evaluation/validation.
A strategy for evaluating training.
Outline of main techniques:

- interview
- questionnaire
- cost-benefit analysis
- testing
- repertory grid
- behaviour observation
- reactionnaire.

Practical work to design an evaluation of current or proposed training.

– Follow-up half-day.

Review of ongoing design work on evaluation projects:
  ● one-to-one coaching
  ● short presentations to the workshop group
  ● tutor input on processing evaluation data.

– Telephone helpline.

This enables workshop members to obtain advice or to resolve queries arising from their project work.

– Final follow-up day.

This follows the period during which workshop members will have implemented the data collection stage of their projects:
  ● a review of progress within each project
  ● tutor inputs on reporting and using evaluation findings
  ● planning for completion of projects
  ● planning for future strategy and evaluation activities.

WORKSHOP 3

Managers' Role in Effective Training

Learning objectives

At the end of the workshop, participants will be able to:

– Describe the key elements of training strategy.
– Review the role of training in contributing to the aims of the organization.
– Offer relevant, collaborative support to corporate training activities.
– Collect validation and evaluation data in the workplace, using evaluation/validation instruments prepared for them.

Topics

What is training strategy about?

– Marketing approach.
– Corporate purposes.
– Manager-trainer collaboration.
– Systematic training design.
– Quality assurance in training.
– Assessing effectiveness.

Outline of main techniques of validation and evaluation

– When is each appropriate?

Exercise: bottom-line penalties of competence gaps.

Exercise: drafting a short behaviour observation checklist to assess the use of a specified aspect of interpersonal skills in the workplace.

Attitudes or Behaviour?

Undue amounts of energy have been expended in training circles over many years on the contentious question of whether training sets out (or should set out) to change the way people behave or the attitudes they hold. My view is strongly on the side of a behavioural focus. I do not doubt that sometimes attitudes shape behaviour (although the reverse is also true), but as a practical person I find it a great economy of effort to work with those features of people which are accessible to guidance and to observation. Second-guessing what is happening in people's heads may be fun but it isn't reliable.

As trainers we can directly influence and observe behaviour; as managers we can see what our staff are doing and can reward good performance, or correct bad. What we cannot do is obtain direct access to the thought processes going on inside other people's heads. We have to rely either on the other person's willingness and capacity for introspection, or on our own guesses, which in turn can only be based on behavioural evidence. The difficulty involved in changing attitudes against the subject's will should be caution enough. Anything more than minor personality change is difficult to achieve and takes a long time. Not least, changes in attitude do not necessarily lead to matching changes in work performance. Furthermore, people can and do behave in ways that contradict the attitudes they hold.

By focusing on observed work behaviour several of the traps that lead to ineffective training are avoided. Identification of training needs starts with such questions as 'What are people doing (or not doing) that needs to be changed?', or 'What would you, the manager, like to *see* people doing differently after they have been trained?'. This kind of analysis sidesteps the trap of stating training needs in terms of the personality traits of an idealized occupant of the job. 'Smith has a lot of trouble getting useful information out of prospects' is a much more useful diagnosis, than statements such as the following: 'Smith needs to be a more outgoing person', or 'Smith is a bit short of motivation'.

A behavioural focus also avoids the trap of talking about 'awareness', a weasel word which suggests training of the 'nice to know' rather than 'need to know' type. It also suggests that no practical consequences should be expected. 'Awareness' events are what you get when the trainer or client is not clear what it is that they are trying to make happen.

'Should objectives be set for "developmental" training?' is a common question. The process of personal development can go in many very different directions and we cannot therefore validate the activity against a criterion of achieving a pre-defined end-state. However, we may wish to make an assessment on a criterion of the use that trainees make of what has been learned.

Using End-of-course Reactions Data

The most commonly-encountered form of training assessment is the end-of-course feedback questionnaire, the 'reactionnaire', or – more perjoratively – the 'happy sheet'. A well-designed reactionnaire will yield some useful though fairly rough-and-ready information to trainers, drawing on trainees' perceptions rather than on objectively-verifiable data:

- How trainees felt about the course.
- Whether particular learning methods were well-received or not.
- Whether or not the trainers were perceived to 'perform' well.
- Whether the event was perceived to match expectations or formally-stated objectives.
- Whether housekeeping arrangements were satisfactory.

However, reactionnaires have major limitations and do not merit detailed coverage as a validation technique. The most significant limits on the technique are that:

- It does not measure learning: at most it gives an indication of whether or not trainees *think* that they have learned something.
- It provides no information on whether or not learning will transfer into the workplace.
- It does not reliably assess the effectiveness of training methods, or the trainers themselves.

6 Statistical Issues in Validation

	SUMMARY	
▷		◁

- The importance of statistics to validation work is explained. Several significant methodological issues are discussed: control groups; sampling; use of descriptive statistics; reliability; and validity. Guidance is provided on how to analyse validation data once they have been collected and how to present them to best effect in formal validation reports.
- The use of statistics in various aspects of validation test design and implementation is outlined: conversion of raw scores to gain ratios; comparing group scores; standard (Z) scores; comparing frequencies; the guessing correction; item analysis.

Why Statistics?

This chapter surveys the main statistical questions that can arise during evaluation projects. The reason for using any particular statistical technique is described; each technique is then presented in step-by-step fashion so that it can be employed by a person with little formal knowledge of statistical methods.

A survey of methodological and statistical issues in validation is necessary for at least two reasons. First, there are certain validation conclusions that you simply cannot arrive at if you do not employ statistical techniques. These are questions where you cannot make any meaningful intuitive assessment (eg, comparing scores attained by two different course groups or calculating whether or not any particular question within a test battery accurately discriminates between good and bad trainees).

Second, appropriate use of statistical techniques helps the trainer to counter the criticism that validation lacks 'rigour'. (Usually, this criticism is advanced cynically in a defensive attempt to avoid the validation process, presenting the spurious argument that information is worthless if it has not been collected under perfectly-controlled conditions.)

Scientific Method

Whilst the methodology adopted for validation studies should be as rigorous as circumstances permit, it has to be recognized that validation is conducted in working organizations, not in the controlled experimental conditions of a laboratory. Often we will have to accept that, by the standards of academic research, we cannot make unqualified claims for the validity of our conclusions. The samples may be too small; control groups may be lacking; there may be substantial reliance on effectively-unverifiable self-report data.

That said, there is a vast difference between asserting your belief that training is working and presenting evidence for that belief, evidence which has been collected as systematically as circumstances allow, offering usable information that decision-makers can act upon. It is a move towards scientific method whenever the influence of 'gut feel' is minimized, and the weight given to carefully-collected evidence is maximized. End-of-course euphoria – whether due to satisfaction or relief – is never a measure of learning nor of its subsequent application. Evaluation by gut feeling has had a long run despite (or perhaps because of) its lack of validity, but it is time that such wholly subjective pseudo-techniques were laid to rest. If the methods we use are to be as good as we can make them, then we need to understand such topics as control groups and sampling, comparing scores, item analysis and so on.

Control Groups

The most convincing evidence that a training activity has worked is that there have been changes (relating to the learning objectives) in the trained group that cannot be found in groups similar in all respects except that they have not been trained. Control groups comprise people who are closely alike in all significant features (eg, age, experience, work history, skills, educational level, sex) to the people in the trained group. Ideally the only difference between the groups is that one gets training and the other doesn't. Control groups should, if possible, be formed by

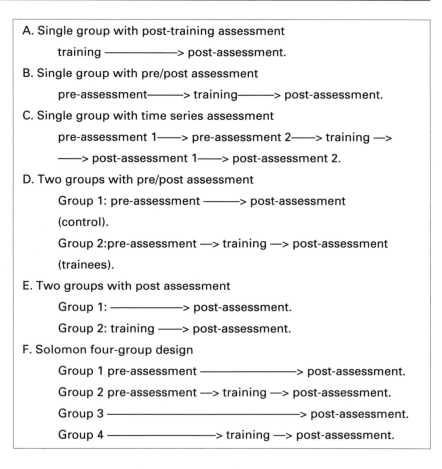

A. Single group with post-training assessment

    training ——————> post-assessment.

B. Single group with pre/post assessment

    pre-assessment——————> training——————> post-assessment.

C. Single group with time series assessment

    pre-assessment 1——————> pre-assessment 2——————> training —>

    ——————> post-assessment 1——————> post-assessment 2.

D. Two groups with pre/post assessment

    Group 1: pre-assessment ——————> post-assessment

    (control).

    Group 2:pre-assessment —> training —> post-assessment

    (trainees).

E. Two groups with post assessment

    Group 1: ——————> post-assessment.

    Group 2: training ——> post-assessment.

F. Solomon four-group design

    Group 1 pre-assessment ——————————> post-assessment.

    Group 2 pre-assessment —> training —> post-assessment.

    Group 3 ——————————————> post-assessment.

    Group 4 ——————————> training —> post-assessment.

Figure 6.1: *Control group designs*

random selection and the identity of members should not be revealed.

In working organizations it is very difficult to prevent contamination of control groups by leakages from people in the trainee group. Sometimes, control groups will be unacceptable on policy grounds (eg, a control group which is prevented from receiving safety training). Control groups may be inappropriate where training concerns a new area of skill or knowledge, such that no comparison is possible with untrained subjects.

Figure 6.1 shows the types of control group arrangement that can be made. Designs A, B and C may be used where no comparison between groups is feasible. If there is clear evidence of changed performance following training, that evidence will for most practical purposes be good enough. Designs D and E offer more comprehensive control.

Type A Control Group

This is satisfactory provided you are sure that the trainees have no knowledge or skill (relevant to the validation) which can be assessed prior to training. A post-test will yield a measure of learning gained during the training. Otherwise, post-assessment offers only a measure of their competence after the event – the training itself may have increased, decreased or had no effect on their performance.

Type B Control Group

This measures learning gain within training. Note that it is possible for the pre-test to have a 'sensitizing' effect on participants by focusing their attention on the key learning tasks. Learning may also have been influenced by external factors such as changes in supervision, the workplace and so on.

Type C Control Group

Here, the trainee group acts as its own control group. A sequence of assessments is made before and after the training event (starting and finishing several months distant from the training itself). This offers some control over external factors.

Type D Control Groups

Two matched groups (one of which receives training) are compared. This controls all non-training variables, but does not provide a control for the effects of testing itself.

Type E Control Groups

An alternative to D uses post-test only, with a control group. This eliminates any effects due to the pre-test, but does not allow measurement of learning within the training itself. It is therefore only appropriate where the subject of the training is wholly new.

Type F Control Groups

This provides the most rigorous control of non-training variables. Four groups are matched in the study, which makes it difficult to achieve outside laboratory conditions. The design controls for the effects of pre-testing on the untrained groups and for the effects of the training programme isolated from any external effects.

Sampling

The purpose of sampling is to reduce the number of people from whom validation data must be collected, whilst remaining confident that the data will be representative of the whole population of trained persons. Social science and market research, both focusing primarily upon opinion data, have been the main sources of theory about sampling, typically basing it upon very large populations. The trainer, by contrast, typically faces a much smaller population from which to draw samples (which, other things being equal, implies a proportionately larger sample size), but is frequently constrained by practical pressures to keep the sample size 'manageable' because of the workload it would create both for validators and respondents.

Sample size needs to be increased the greater the variations between members of the population; or in the absence of control groups; or where the training activities produce only small measurable differences. The larger the population, the more people that are required in the sample, but the smaller the sample needs to be as a proportion of the population. Variability within the population is measured in terms of standard deviation (SD), estimated from previous studies or a pilot or from knowledge of the activity under study. Where the range of possible scores is already known (unusual in a training context), SD can be estimated adequately by dividing the range by six (because, for a normal distribution, six SDs will account for more than 99 per cent of the range).

On the other hand, stratification of the population (on some relevant criterion) into sub-populations, each of which can be individually sampled, allows the trainer to reduce sample size. Such stratification might be made according to length of service, prior qualifications, age, full-time vs. part-time employment and like factors.

Sampling is usually 'random', that is, each person in the population has an equal chance of selection. The rationale for random sampling is to obtain findings that can be generalized to the whole population. However, where the quality of the ideas that respondents give is the main consideration, then a 'purposive' sample with deliberate, careful selection of who is to be included may be appropriate.

Sample size can be arrived at through statistical textbook formulae calculation or by adopting a more pragmatic rule-of-thumb basis which relies on sample size guidelines in published studies. Smith[3] provides a useful survey of sample sizes in a number of evaluation projects. A more comprehensive survey of sampling and statistical issues is provided in my forthcoming book on training strategy and evaluation.[4]

Certain validation techniques lend themselves to smaller sample sizes than others, irrespective of the population size. For example, when using interview or behaviour observation, a sample of around 20–30 subjects is usually quite adequate and more respondents usually simply means diminishing returns of information. The sample sizes in Table 6.1) are suggested for the data collection techniques listed.

TECHNIQUE	NO.IN SAMPLE
Behaviour observation (trained observer)	15
Behaviour observation (line supervisor)	50
Test of knowledge	30
Practical test	30
Critical incident method	50
Interview	30

Adapted from Smith, 1980.[3]

Table 6.1 *Validation techniques and sample sizes*

Analysing the Data

The trainer needs to summarize and analyse the validation data that have been collected.Otherwise, they lie around in large piles attracting dust and cynicism. It is essential right at the start of the project design to pose the question of how you intend to analyse the data that you are about to collect. Design validation instruments so that it is easy to read off the responses. If your computer system permits it and the material consists of closed multiple-choice-type items, consider the use of bar codes printed alongside test answers; linked to a suitable statistical package, you can benefit from rapid data analysis and summary of results.

In the case of test material, the data summary will usually consist of the test score itself, compiled via the marking scheme, and further analysis may then be applied to compare individual or group scores or to measure the effectiveness of the test items themselves.

In the case of data collected by methods such as interview or critical incident the summary of data may be a matter of adding up the total responses of each type (but it often is rather less straightforward). More usually, the first step is for the raw data provided by respondents to be sorted and classified. The way you classify the answers must reflect the reasons for asking the question.

The categories must meet two criteria:

- there must be no overlap of meaning or content between one category and another and no ambiguity about the boundaries between categories;
- the set of categories for each question must cover every possible acceptable response (this is often covered by including an 'other – please specify' option within the categories).

Categorizing responses to open questions sometimes causes difficulties to validators. Start by categorizing one or two tapes (or response sheets) and then get someone else to analyse the same raw data; compare interpretations and categorizations. Use respondents' own words as a stepping stone to categorization – and be careful not to distort the subjects' views through over-simplification or by imposing (consciously or not) your own opinions. Next, you should group the key words and phrases that you have identified into internally-consistent categories that you can use in the data matrix.

Where more than one person is classifying the raw data, it is essential that each categorizes the same data in the same way, ie, that 'inter-coder reliability' is achieved. Scope for individual interpretation during data analysis must be eliminated and coders trained to understand the meaning of each question and the acceptable response options. Never ignore any differences of interpretation between one person's categorization and another's – such differences usually reflect different, as yet unidentified, categories.

Only when classification and sorting has been completed can you proceed to frequency counts and statistical analyses. The data matrix provides a framework for the categorization. At its simplest, the matrix summarizes the number of identical (or closely similar) responses to each question (see, for example Table 6.2).

Question:	Did you receive any pre-course briefing?	
Responses:	Briefing by manager	8
	Briefing by training department	15
	Briefing by other person	3
	No briefing received	6
(Assumes that 32 questionnaires were returned)		

Table 6.2 *A simple data matrix*

The matrix can be made more complex and the analysis can be made more informative by using a matrix which distinguishes the types of respondent as well as their response categories (see, for example, 6.3 and 6.4).

Question:	How many months have you been employed in your present job?			
	Less than 12	12–35	36–59	60+
	4	5	4	8

Table 6.3 *A more complex data matrix (a)*

Question:	Please indicate the extent of any briefing that subordinates receive before attending training events.	
Responses:	I brief them	9
	Someone else briefs them	5
	No briefing is given	7

The two examples above can then be combined into a single matrix such as that shown in Table 6.5

Table 6.4 *A more complex data matrix (b)*

Response categories	Length of Service (months)			
	Under 12	12–35	36–59	60+
Manager provides briefing	4	3	1	1
Other person provides briefing	0	0	2	3
No briefing provided	0	2	1	4

Table 6.5 *A combined data matrix*

Descriptive Statistics

Sometimes validation data can be used without further statistical analysis, as descriptive case studies or as simple reports of test scores; often, however, it is useful to apply statistical analysis in order to make statements about how 'typical', how 'varied', etc. the findings are. It is outside the scope of this book to explain in detail how to make these various calculations and the information is readily available in most basic text-books on the subject. The types of descriptive statistic that may be useful in validation studies are as follows:

- Measures of what is 'typical' of the sample:
    - if the category has been measured on an *equal interval* scale then the arithmetic mean is appropriate;
    - if the response categories can be put in *order of magnitude*, but do not form an equal interval scale, the median (midpoint value) should be used;
    - If the response categories do not form a true scale from lesser to greater, but a *nominal scale* (or pseudo-scale) as, for example, with multiple-choice alternatives, the proper measure is the mode (or most frequent value).
- Measures of how widely individual people or cases within a group vary from the 'average':
    - the extremes of the variation are shown by the range;
    - quartile deviation (based on the median) shows those points within which the central half of cases fall.
    - the average deviation of any individual case from the group mean is calculated using the formula for standard deviation.
- Measures of how individual cases are distributed in relation to another variable:
    - graphing the distribution curve which may reveal the 'normal' bell-shaped curve, an asymmetrically-skewed pattern, or a straight-line relationship.
- Measures of the way in which changes in one or more variables produce changes in another variable:
    - calculation of the Pearson correlation coefficient.
- Measures of the differences between sets of frequencies (such as test results, occurrences of behaviour, etc.):
    - application of the chi-squared test to the data.
- Measure of the limitations of generalizing from a sample to the population from which it has been drawn:
    - tests of significance.

The Validation Report

The purpose of putting your findings into a report is to get people to read it and to act on it. Clear, concise, plain English should be the rule. Avoid formality or pseudo-academicism: there should be no doubt about what the report says and what the implications are. Facts and opinions should be clearly distinguished. A suggested framework for the report follows:

- *Contents* listing and any general *Preface* (eg, an endorsement from a senior manager).
- Brief summary of the main *Conclusions and Recommendations*. (This is all that some people will ever read).
- A summary of *Project Details*: who commissioned it, which training activity has been validated, what technique(s) have been employed and who has conducted the study.
- The *Main Text* of the report, comprising:
  - a summary of each finding;
  - commentary on that finding;
  - proposals for action.
- *Concluding Remarks*: these may include general comments about the validation process in that organization; observations on how worthwhile the study has been; and exhortations to managers to mend their wicked ways.
- *Appendices*: depending on how much detailed information you wish to impose on your audience (and also on the impression of 'substance' that you want to create) you may opt to include methodological descriptions and raw data in the document. Optional appendix material may include:
  - a description of data-gathering techniques with copies of the instruments used; details of sample size and similar technical information;
  - the raw data from which the analytical summaries have been drawn (but note here the importance of maintaining any guarantees of anonymity you have given to respondents);
  - extended case studies based upon the data.

Reporting validation studies is not the final step in the training cycle. Information without action is futile. The next task is to build support for the changes you have proposed. Useful questions to ask are:

- Who might benefit from the proposals?
- What are the financial payoffs from the proposals?
- What are the formal lines of authority on your proposal?
- What obstacles can you anticipate?
- What can you do to work around such obstacles?

Remember that validation data will give you a rational foundation for promoting changes but the process of achieving them remains a political game, with all the usual vested interests, competition for resources, lobbying and use of the informal structure of communications and influence.

Statistics in Testing

Raw Scores and Gain Ratios

The pre- and post- scores achieved in tests by each member of a group of trainees provides a measure of individual learning gain, but no basis for comparing learning gain across the group, because each trainee may be starting from a different level of performance. Gain ratios make such comparisons possible by converting raw scores into percentages that measure actual attainment against the room for improvement that existed pre-training. The formula is as follows:

$$\frac{\text{post- score } \textit{minus} \text{ pre- score}}{\text{maximum score } \textit{minus} \text{ pre- score}} \times 100 = \text{Gain Ratio } \%$$

Thus, a trainee with pre- and post-scores of 50 and 80 (from 100 maximum) achieves a gain ratio of 60 per cent; another trainee, with nominally the same improvement in score, from 30 to 60, shows a lower gain ratio of 43 per cent.

Comparing Group Scores

It is sometimes necessary to compare the scores achieved on one test by either different groups or by the same group at different times. Calculation of the standard deviation of scores within each group will show the extent to which scores are spread around the group mean (the arithmetical average). The formula for standard deviation is:

$$\text{SD} = \sqrt{\frac{\text{sum of squares of individual deviations from mean of group}}{\text{number of items}}}$$

Standard (Z) Scores

Where results need to be compared from different tests which may not be directly comparable, the technique to use is the Z-score conversion, amended (by setting the mean at 50 and each standard deviation at 10) to eliminate negative scores. The formula is:

$$\text{Amended Z-score} = \frac{50 + 10(\text{raw score } \textit{minus} \text{ mean})}{\text{standard deviation}}$$

Comparing Frequencies

Sometimes you may need to compare two groups not on the levels of score they have attained but in terms of the frequency with which some feature of the test occurs, eg, the pass rates for different learning methods. The technique for this analysis is the chi-squared test. The formula for the chi-squared test is as follows:

where O = observed frequency and E = a frequency which could be expected on the basis of some likely hypothesis about the subject matter.

It is outside the scope of this book to give a detailed illustration of the extended calculation involved, but the information is readily available in statistics textbooks.

The Guessing Correction

A multiple-choice question with four equally-convincing possible answers carries the risk that 25 per cent of correct answers may be the result of guesses; for simple true/false alternatives, there is a 50 per cent chance of correct guessing. There have been a number of proposals to make allowance for possible guesses by penalizing wrong answers more than unanswered items, though no system can distinguish between correct guesses and genuine knowledge, nor between wrong guesses and genuine errors.

The adjustments suggested here are derived from Akeroyd.[5] In the case of a four-option multiple-choice question, marks are allocated as follows:

Correct answer = 1 mark.
Two answers selected, one of which is correct = 1/2 mark.
No answer = 1/4 mark.
Incorrect answer = 0 mark.

With true/false items, a simpler formula can be applied:

Corrected score = number of *minus* number of
correct wrong
answers answers

111

Reliability

Reliability refers both to the consistency with which test items measure performance and to the consistency of the testers' judgements (particularly important when applied to behaviour observation). A reliable test is one that produces the same score results when administered to the same group of people on different occasions (assuming that their knowledge has not changed in the intervening period). It indicates that differences in an individual's scores are the result of real changes (such as training) rather than chance fluctuations in the testing process itself.

Test reliability can be increased quite simply, by:

– longer tests which provide a more comprehensive coverage of the training that is being validated;
– pre-tested, clear instructions on test completion;
– standardization of test conditions, duration and such matters as guidance of trainees;
– standardisation of scoring with training of test scorers.

Reliability is measured by the degree of variation between two sets of test scores, given as the correlation coefficient within a range from +1 to -1. Typical real levels fall somewhere between 0 and +1. Perfect correlation is indicated by +1.00; one set of scores is a perfect predictor of a second set of scores on the same test: the test is totally consistent or reliable. A correlation of -1.00 indicates that the individual who scores best on the first occasion will score worst on the second use of the test. A correlation of 0 means that test scores are random.

Reliability coefficients can be calculated in several ways: for training applications, the split-half method is advised, which treats two halves of a test (usually odd- and even-numbered items) as if they were independent applications of the whole test; the Pearson product moment correlation coefficient is the formula to use here:

where n = number of trainees, X = odd number scores and Y = even number scores.

Validity

Validity is concerned with whether or not the test provides an assessment of what it is meant to. This is something to be determined by subject experts, having reference to each particular application. 'Content-validity' is the extent that the test provides representative and balanced coverage of the objectives of the training. 'Face-validity' is the issue of whether trainees perceive the test to be a valid representation of the training; as such, it is more a presentational issue than a technical one. Nevertheless, face-validity is important as a determinant of the test's acceptability, perceived fairness and credibility. Face-validity can often be increased by making the language of a test item more congruent with the language and/or literacy skills of the trainees, or by re-writing items to place them in contexts with which the trainees can identify.

Item Analysis

Individual test items can be assessed in terms of a) facility values (FV) and b) the index of discrimination (ID). The facility value is a measure of how difficult a test item is to answer. The degree of difficulty is expressed by the proportion of trainees who correctly answer the test item. The ID is a measure of whether an item distinguishes reliably between good and bad trainees.

To calculate the FV for a multiple-choice test item, the formula is:

$$FV = \frac{\text{number of trainees giving correct answer}}{\text{total number of trainees tested}}$$

The result should be calculated to two decimal places. For criterion-referenced tests the FV should be 0.70 or higher: the expectation is that most trainees will achieve the 'pass' standard. (Note, too, that high FVs mean that the item will necessarily show a low ID scoring and vice versa).

Low FVs indicate very difficult items where it is often as easy to score correctly by guessing. For example, a four-option multiple-choice item presents a 25 per cent chance that a guess will be correct. If the item has an FV of 0.20, then a guess offers better odds of being right.

The calculation of ID requires that a tested group is divided into three categories: the top 27 per cent, the bottom 27 per cent and the middle 46 per cent, based upon overall performance in the test (ie, not based on the results of any single test item). The next step is to tabulate the results for each test item, broken down into the three sub-groups. In a multiple choice example, this tabulation will show how many in each sub-group answered each of the possible answers to a given item. ID is then calculated as the proportion of the top 27 per cent who gave the correct answer minus the proportion of the bottom 27 per cent who also gave the correct answer. A low ID, 0.30 or less, indicates that trainees who scored poorly overall on the test were just as likely as the trainees who scored well overall to perform well on that particular item within the test. A negative ID means that poor trainees are scoring better on the item than good trainees.

Notes

1   Bramley, P and Newby, AC (1984) 'The Evaluation of Training; *Journal of European Industrial Training*, vol 8, nos 6–7.

2   This approach was developed in my 1985 training package 'TEAM – the Training Audit Evaluation Method'. It will appear in revised form in the forthcoming title from Gower Publishing *The Training Evaluation Handbook* (Autumn 1992).

3   Smith, ME (1980) 'How big a sample do I need for my evaluation?' *Performance Instruction*, vol 11, no 10, pp. 3–10.

4   Newby, AC. (1992, forthcoming).

5   Akeroyd, M (1982) *Journal of Further & Higher Education*, vol 6, no 3.

6   Kelly, G (1955) *The Psychology of Personal Consultants*, NY, Norton.

Index

analyzing validation data *see* data analysis *and* statistics and validation
assessment criteria, use of appropriate 16
attitudes and behaviour 43–4, 98–9
attitudes, measurement of 67 seq

behaviour and attitudes *see* attitudes and behaviour
behaviour categories, selection of 49 seq
behaviour observation instruments 44 seq
behaviour observation technique
    behaviour categories, selection of 49 seq
    behaviour observation instruments 44
    critical incident diary 54 seq
    design of instruments 47 seq
    feedback after testing 91
    introduction 43
    methods 46
    overview 30
    rating errors by observers 89–90
    reliability 90
    resistance to observation 45
    self-report methods 53 seq
    training to use the technique 88 seq

classification of skill levels 77–8
closed and open book tests 33, 85
comparing group scores 110
comparing scoring frequencies 111
competences and validation 17
completion items for written tests 39
consultants, use of specialist validation 18
control groups 101 seq

criterion and norm-referenced testing 85–6
Critical Incident Review technique
    analysis of data 55 seq
    diary format 54 seq
    overview 29

data analysis
    critical incident data 55
    data matrix 106–7
    general 28,105
    interview data 65 seq
    Repertory Grid, 74
    statistics *see* statistics and validation
data matrix 106–7
descriptive statistics 107
design of behaviour observation instruments 47 seq
design of interview schedule 57
design of practical tests 83 seq

end-of-course reactions data 99
essay as test method 40
evaluation and validation 10

facility values 113
feedback to trainees after testing 91
frequency statements 65–6

gain ratios 33, 91, 110
guessing correction 111

happy sheets 99

index of discrimination 113

116

illustrative insights from validation interview 65
inter-coder reliability 106
interpersonal skills training, validation of 43 seq
     see behaviour observation, Critical Incident
     Review, interview, Repertory Grid
intervention strategy using validation 16
interview technique
    analyzing interview data 64 seq
    conducting the interview 63,64
    designing the interview schedule 57
    frequency statements 65, 66
    illustrative insights 65
    introduction 56
    overview 28
    tape recording 62, 63
    training for validation interviewing 91–3
in-tray tests 82
item analysis 113

knowledge tests
    applications 31
    designing knowledge tests 34
    open and closed book tests 33
    recall/supply items
        completion items 37
        essay 38
        short answer 39
    recognition items
        matching items 41
        multiple-choice questions 39
        true/false questions 40
    resistance to testing 32
    test banks 34
    training of testers 90–91
    types of test item 33

managers' validation workshops 93–4, 97–8
matching items for written tests 41
multiple choice questions 39

norm and criterion-referenced testing 85

observation methods 46
observation paranoia 45
open and closed book tests 33, 85

overview of this book 11

performance deficiencies 14
politics in organizations and validation 20
practical test technique
    administration of tests 86–7
    classifying skill levels 77–8
    closed and open book tests 85
    designing the practical test 83 seq
    feedback after testing 91
    in-tray tests 82
    introduction 76
    manual dexterity items 83
    norm and criterion-referenced tests 85–6
    overview 30
    procedure-following items 81
    problem-solving and analytical items 82–3
    recall and identification items 78 seq
    safety 83 seq
    training of testers 90–91
professional self-esteem of trainers 16

quality control of training 15
question types in validation interviewing 58 seq

rating errors by observers 89–90
reliability
    in behaviour observation 90
    in testing 112
reactions data at end of course 99
Repertory Grid technique
    analyzing the data 74
    analysis form 68
    introduction 67
    overview 29
    using the technique 69 seq
reporting validation findings 108
resistance to observation 45
resistance to testing 32

safety in testing 83 seq, 90
sampling 22, 104
scientific method 101
self-report methods
    critical incident diary 54 seq

interview 56 seq
short answer items in written testing 41
standard (Z) scores 110
statistics and validation
    analyzing the data 105
    comparing group scores 110
    comparing frequencies 111
    control groups 101 seq
    data matrix 106–7
    descriptive statistics 107
    facility values 113
    gain ratios 33, 91, 110
    guessing correction 111
    index of discrimination 113
    inter-coder reliability 106
    item analysis 113
    reliability in tests 112
    sampling 104
    scientific method 101
    standard (Z) scores 110
    validity in testing 113
    why use statistics? 100
tape recording of interviews 62–3
technique and project implementation workshop 96–7
techniques for validation, choice of 25 seq
test banks 34
tests of knowledge *see* knowledge tests
trainers and managers
    training workshop 93–4, 97–8
    using validation as intervention strategy 16
training cycle 17 seq
training design, efficient 15
training trainers in validation skills
    behaviour observation 88–90

interviewing 91–3
testing 90–91
techniques and project implementation workshop 96–7
trainers and managers 93 seq
training needs, nature of 13
true/false questions 40

validation
    and competences 17
    and evaluation 10
    as intervention strategy 16
    choice of technique 25 seq
    consultants, use of 18
    data analysis *see* data analysis
    how much is needed? 21
    is it necessary? 15
    organizational context 18, 20
    politics 20, 22
    pre/post measurement 24, 27
    projects, design of 22 seq
    sampling 22, 104
    techniques overview 28 seq
    track record of success 16
    training trainers to use validation 20, 88 seq
    what it is 9, 10, 18
    within the training cycle 17 seq
    why validate training? 13
validity in testing 113

why use statistics? 100
who is this book for? 9
written test technique *see* knowledge tests

Z–scores 110